W9-BYZ-305

JOHN C. CALHOUN

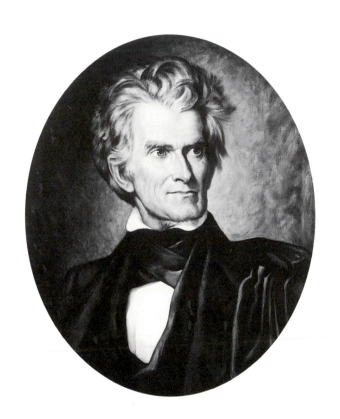

THE CHELSEA HOUSE LIBRARY OF BIOGRAPHY

JOHN C. CALHOUN

WARREN BROWN

Chelsea House Publishers

New York • Philadelphia

CHELSEA HOUSE PUBLISHERS

Editor-in-Chief   Richard S. Papale
Executive Managing Editor   Karyn Gullen Browne
Copy Chief   Philip Koslow
Picture Editor   Adrian Allen
Art Director   Nora Wertz
Manufacturing Director   Gerald Levine
Systems Manager   Lindsey Ottman
Production Coordinator   Marie Claire Cebrián-Ume

The Chelsea House Library of Biography
Senior Editor   Kathy Kuhtz

Staff for **John C. Calhoun**
Text Editor   Marian W. Taylor
Copy Editor   Margaret Dornfeld
Editorial Assistant   Laura Petermann
Picture Researcher   Pat Burns
Series Designer   Basia Niemczyc
Cover Illustration   Robert Caputo

Copyright © 1993 by Chelsea House Publishers, a division of Main Line Book Co. All rights reserved.

Printed and bound in Mexico.

First Printing

1   3   5   7   9   8   6   4   2

Library of Congress Cataloging-in-Publication Data

Brown, Warren, 1963–
John C. Calhoun/Warren Brown.
p. cm.—(The Chelsea House library of biography)
Includes bibliographical references and index.
Summary: Examines the life and career of the nineteenth-century politician.
ISBN 0-7910-1727-3
      0-7910-1728-1 (pbk.)
1. Calhoun, John C. (John Caldwell), 1782–1850—Juvenile literature. 2. Legis-
lators—United States—Biography—Juvenile literature. 3. United States. Con-
gress. Senate—Biography—Juvenile literature. [1. Calhoun, John C. (John
Caldwell), 1782–1850. 2. Statesmen.] I. Title. II. Series.
E340.C15B76 1993   92-24366
328.73'092—dc20   CIP
[B]   AC

Contents

THE CHELSEA HOUSE LIBRARY OF BIOGRAPHY

Other titles in the series are forthcoming.

Introduction

Learning from Biographies

Vito Perrone

The oldest narratives that exist are biographical. Much of what we know, for example, about the Pharaohs of ancient Egypt, the builders of Babylon, the philosophers of Greece, the rulers of Rome, the many biblical and religious leaders who provide the base for contemporary spiritual beliefs, has come to us through biographies—the stories of their lives. Although an oral tradition was long the mainstay of historically important biographical accounts, the oral stories making up this tradition became by the 1st century A.D. central elements of a growing written literature.

In the 1st century A.D., biography assumed a more formal quality through the work of such writers as Plutarch, who left us more than 500 biographies of political and intellectual leaders of Rome and Greece. This tradition of focusing on great personages lasted well into the 20th century and is seen as an important means of understanding the history of various times and places. We learn much, for example, from Plutarch's writing about the collapse of the Greek city-states and about the struggles in Rome over the justice and the constitutionality of a world empire. We also gain considerable understanding of the definitions of morality and civic virtue and how various common men and women lived out their daily existence.

Not surprisingly, the earliest American writing, beginning in the 17th century, was heavily biographical. Those Europeans who came to America were dedicated to recording their experience, especially the struggles they faced in building what they determined to be a new culture. John Norton's *Life and Death of John Cotton*, printed in 1630, typifies these early works. Later biographers often tackled more ambitious projects. Cotton Mather's *Magnalia Christi Americana*, published in 1702, accounted for the lives of more than 70 ministers and political leaders. In addition, a biographical literature around the theme of Indian captivity had considerable popularity. Soon after the American Revolution and the organization of the United States of America, Americans were treated to a large outpouring of biographies about such figures as Benjamin Franklin, George Washington, Thomas Jefferson, and Aaron Burr, among others. These particular works served to build a strong sense of national identity.

Among the diverse forms of historical literature, biographies have been over many centuries the most popular. And in recent years interest in biography has grown even greater, as biography has gone beyond prominent government figures, military leaders, giants of business, industry, literature, and the arts. Today we are treated increasingly to biographies of more common people who have inspired others by their particular acts of courage, by their positions on important social and political issues, or by their dedicated lives as teachers, town physicians, mothers, and fathers. Through this broader biographical literature, much of which is featured in the CHELSEA HOUSE LIBRARY OF BIOGRAPHY, our historical understandings can be enriched greatly.

What makes biography so compelling? Most important, biography is a human story. In this regard, it makes of history something personal, a narrative with which we can make an intimate connection. Biographers typically ask us as readers to accompany them on a journey through the life of another person, to see some part of the world through another's eyes. We can, as a result, come to understand what it is like to live the life of a slave, a farmer, a textile worker, an engineer, a poet, a president—in a sense, to walk in another's shoes. Such experience can be personally invaluable. We cannot ask for a better entry into historical studies.

Although our personal lives are likely not as full as those we are reading about, there will be in most biographical accounts many common experiences. As with the principal character of any biography, we are also faced with numerous decisions, large and small. In the midst of living our lives we are not usually able to comprehend easily the significance of our daily decisions or grasp easily their many possible consequences, but we can gain important insights into them by seeing the decisions made by others play themselves out. We can learn from others.

Because biography is a personal story, it is almost always full of surprises. So often, the personal lives of individuals we come across historically are out of view, their public personas masking who they are. It is through biography that we gain access to their private lives, to the acts that define who they are and what they truly care about. We see their struggles within the possibilities and limitations of life, gaining insight into their beliefs, the ways they survived hardships, what motivated them, and what discouraged them. In the process we can come to understand better our own struggles.

As you read this biography, try to place yourself within the subject's world. See the events as that person sees them. Try to understand why the individual made particular decisions and not others. Ask yourself if you would have chosen differently. What are the values or beliefs that guide the subject's actions? How are those values or beliefs similar to yours? How are they different from yours? Above all, remember: You are engaging in an important historical inquiry as you read a biography, but you are also reading a literature that raises important personal questions for you to consider.

*John Caldwell Calhoun, who sat for this daguerreotype by Mathew B.
Brady in the 1840s, was the voice and conscience of the pre–Civil War
South. An impassioned orator, author, and defender of states' rights
and slavery, the South Carolinian served as a congressman, a senator,
and vice-president of the United States.*

1

The Final Crisis

EVERYBODY WHO WAS ANYBODY was there. On March 4, 1850, politicians, social leaders, bankers, lawyers, doctors, bishops, judges—all the elite of Washington, D.C.—seemed headed for the same destination: the Capitol, home of the United States Congress.

The Washingtonians expected to witness some high drama. It had been strongly rumored that today, the legendary—and mortally ill—John C. Calhoun of South Carolina would rise from his sickbed and address the Senate on a matter of national life and death: the admission of California to the Union. All over the city, in offices, drawing rooms, and taverns, no one had talked of much besides the mighty senator and his speech.

As they climbed Capitol Hill on this bright and breezy Monday, the visitors could look down and see the federal city stretched out before them. To the northwest, the broad, tree-lined expanse of Pennsylvania Avenue ran toward the Treasury Building and the White House, then occupied by President Zachary Taylor. To the west lay a long meadow:

Washingtonians gather at the base of Capitol Hill about 1850. On March 4 of that year, the federal city's residents thronged to the Capitol to watch the legendary John C. Calhoun deliver the most historically significant speech of his long career.

the Mall, which extended from the base of Capitol Hill to the red sandstone towers of the unfinished Smithsonian Institution. The Washington Monument, still under construction, was taking shape at the end of the Mall, above the Potomac River.

As the crowd neared the Capitol, Calhoun was leaving his ground-floor room in nearby Hill's boardinghouse, leaning heavily on the arm of an old friend, former South Carolina governor James Hamilton. Physically frail or not, the 77-year-old Calhoun remained the most politically powerful southerner in America. Along with two other human dynamos—senators Henry Clay of Kentucky and Daniel Webster of Massachusetts—he had dominated national politics for most of the 19th century.

But for the past three months, Calhoun had been fighting a losing battle with ill health. Reporting that he had pulmonary pneumonia, a Philadelphia newspaper said he looked "pale and ghastly," and that he seemed "too weak even to hold a pen." Many old Washington hands believed that today's speech, scheduled for the Senate's one o'clock session, would be the old man's last.

For that reason alone, Washingtonians, whether they admired Calhoun or detested him—no one felt neutral— would have flocked to hear the address. But there was more: Calhoun's subject would be larger than California; it would deal with nothing less than the future of slavery— and of the nation itself.

The United States had acquired California after winning the Mexican War in 1848, two years earlier. With the encouragement of President Taylor, California's residents had subsequently drafted a state constitution, which prohibited slavery within its borders. Now, they wished to be admitted to the Union as a free state.

California's request had stirred profound anxiety in the southern states: approval would amount to the banning of slavery from the most fertile part of the territories gained from Mexico. Even more important, the admission to the Union of another free state would upset the balance of political power between the 15 free states—those that prohibited slavery—and the 15 slave states, where human bondage was protected by law.

Behind the immediate issue of California's constitution lay a bitter controversy over slavery in the territories— areas that belonged to the United States but that had not yet achieved statehood. Northerners asserted that slavery, as a moral evil, must not be admitted into the territories, and that the federal government had the right to prohibit it. Most southerners, on the other hand, regarded slavery as a necessary basic institution.

The controversy threatened to split the country in two. In the South, even responsible leaders said that if California was admitted and slavery prohibited in the territories, it would be time for the South to secede from the Union. Mississippi politicians had gone so far as to suggest a southern state convention to decide the secession question. The idea fell on fertile ground; the convention was scheduled to meet in Nashville, Tennessee, in June 1850.

In the North, meanwhile, abolitionists were holding fiery, well-attended public meetings in every community; northern citizens demanded that slavery be barred from the territories and abolished in the District of Columbia. As the year 1850 began, then, the nation found itself in a mood of hair-trigger tension.

Would the American Union die only 74 years after its glorious birth?

No! said moderate citizens and lovers of the Union. Among these passionate Americans was Henry Clay, the feisty but diplomatic Kentucky senator known as the Great Pacificator. To end the "California Crisis" and restore regional peace, Clay proposed to offer the North two major concessions: admission of California as a free state, and abolition of the slave trade in the District of Columbia. To appease the South, New Mexico and Utah (the remaining areas gained from Mexico) would be established as U.S. territories with no restrictions upon slavery; their populations would decide the issue later, when they applied for statehood.

Under Clay's plan, the South would also get a promise of no federal interference with the slaves already in the District of Columbia and no federal regulation of the interstate slave trade. Most important to the South, Clay proposed a tough federal fugitive slave law. The new statute would mandate the arrest and return of runaway slaves, and would impose harsh penalties on anyone who helped a slave escape in any state.

Calhoun's March 4 Senate address would reveal his position on Clay's compromise. No one knew what he would say, but everybody had a guess. Some insisted that the South Carolinian would flatly reject the proposal. After all, they said, he had spent most of his political life battling federal interference with the rights of the southern states; furthermore, they asserted, Calhoun would never put up with any federal restrictions on slavery. Other knowledgable Washingtonians maintained that Calhoun's unquestioned love for the Union would overcome these objections and lead him to support the compromise.

As one o'clock approached, senators and spectators alike waited on the edge of their seats to hear what Calhoun would say; the packed Senate chamber fairly crackled with suspense. Much depended on Calhoun's position: if he favored Clay's compromise, the crisis might yet be defused; the United States of America might continue to exist. If not, the divisive war, whose dark shadow had long haunted both North and South, would loom perilously close.

Now the 59 senators (a pair from each of the Union's 30 states, minus an absentee from Texas) took their places. They sat at wooden desks arranged in a semicircle around the raised seat of Vice-President Millard Fillmore, president of the Senate. As government officials and reporters scrambled for seats in the Senate gallery, elegantly dressed Washington women ignored Senate rules and took over every vacant seat on the floor. Overlooking the somewhat chaotic proceedings was a large bronze eagle, symbol of the young republic.

Suddenly, the buzzing crowd fell silent. Calhoun, still supported by his friend Hamilton, slowly entered the chamber. The old senator's appearance shocked those who had not seen him since the beginning of his illness. Pneumonia had left his normally rugged frame shrunken and emaciated, and he walked with short, feeble steps. His famous lion's mane of hair had turned almost entirely white; deep hollows shadowed his square-jawed face. Nevertheless, noted a reporter from the *Charleston Courier*, the glow in Calhoun's gray eyes indicated that "his heart [was] as firm as ever."

Both friends and antagonists stood to greet the senator as he made his way across the floor. Taking his place—a desk between those of senators James Whitcomb of Indiana and Jefferson Davis of Mississippi—Calhoun tightened his cloak around his bony shoulders and waited for the session to begin.

Senators, not always famed for their exquisite courtesy, had been known to rustle papers, move around, and even chat while fellow members spoke. Not today: when John C. Calhoun rose from his chair, recalled one witness, "the galleries were hushed into the deepest silence." No one stirred, no one spoke, no one seemed even to breathe. "The

Kentuckian Henry Clay, known as the Great Pacificator and Handsome Harry of the West, inspired strong feelings. To his admirers, he was a brilliant, flexible, farseeing statesman, but his detractors called him "a sly, rubber-footed rascal." Equally ambivalent about each other, Clay and Calhoun alternately battled and embraced during the four decades of their intimate political relationship.

hand of death lay heavily on his shoulder," wrote an early Calhoun biographer of this moment, "so that the tears involuntarily pressed into the eyes of those who remembered what an image of strong and noble manhood he had been."

Despite his weakness, Calhoun pulled himself erect and faced his colleagues proudly. "As much indisposed as I have been," he said in a clear, firm voice, "I have felt it to be my duty to express to you my sentiments upon the great question which has agitated the country and occupied your attention." Then, after formally thanking the Senate for "permitting" him to express his views, he handed his already-printed speech to a friend, Senator James Mason of Virginia, to read aloud.

"I have, senators, believed from the first that the agitation of the subject of slavery would, if not prevented by some timely and effective measure, end in disunion," read

Senator Daniel Webster of Massachusetts (right, with his hand raised) responds to the March 4, 1850, speech of Senator John C. Calhoun (circled) on California's admission to the Union. Presiding over the chamber from his desk below the eagle (center) is Vice-President Millard Fillmore.

Mason. "It can no longer be disguised or denied that the Union is in danger. You have thus had forced upon you the greatest and the gravest question that can ever come under your consideration—How can the Union be preserved?"

Calhoun, his words delivered by Mason, then went on to answer that question. He described an impossible scenario. The Union, he asserted, could not exist without perfect balance between North and South; to preserve that Union, the North would have to admit that the South had equal rights in the territories, stop the abolitionist movement, obey the fugitive slave laws, and accept a constitutional amendment forever guaranteeing equality between itself and the South. Unless the South, beset and unfairly treated by the North for many years, received justice, he insisted, the Union would fall to pieces.

Supporters of the Union—probably almost everyone present in the Senate that day—felt their spirits sink lower with each word. Calhoun had damned Clay's compromise and supplanted it with a fantastic set of demands the North never would or could agree to.

Calhoun's closing words gave the final blow to all hopes for lasting tranquility between North and South. Addressing the North, the senator said: "If you, who represent the stronger portion, cannot agree to settle [the differences] on the broad principles of justice and duty, say so; and let the States we both represent agree to separate and part in peace. If you are unwilling we should depart in peace, tell us so, and we shall know what to do, when you reduce the question to submission or resistance."

Congress eventually enacted Clay's plan, known as the Compromise of 1850, but it was too late for the South. Calhoun's stubborn defense of his gallant, bewitchingly beautiful world had helped to doom it. On April 12, 1861, 11 years and 5 months after his final speech in the Senate, Confederate guns opened fire on the federal garrison at Fort Sumter, South Carolina. Twenty-four hours later, Yankees and Rebels began to slaughter one another. The American Civil War had begun.

*This miniature portrait of John Calhoun's father, Patrick, is dated
1791, the year in which Patrick celebrated his 63rd birthday and John
his 9th. Arriving in America in 1733, Irish-born Patrick grew up to be
a strong-willed, outspoken citizen who demanded his rights and taught
young John to do the same.*

2

A Backwoods Genius

JOHN CALDWELL CALHOUN WAS born on March 18, 1782, in the Long Canes region of northwestern South Carolina. He was the fourth child and third son of Patrick Calhoun and his third wife, Martha Caldwell Calhoun.

Scots-descended, Irish-born Patrick Calhoun was five years old when he and his family immigrated to America in 1733. The Calhouns settled in western Pennsylvania, where the colonial government gave free land to anyone who would help defend the colony's western frontier against its French and Indian foes.

In Pennsylvania, the Calhouns struggled with the land, the weather, and constant attacks from the Indians whose former territory they occupied. Life on a frontier farm was hard, but the family found comfort in its religion, a stern Presbyterianism whose believers viewed life as a continuous struggle against evil. Hardworking and devout, the Calhouns accepted the Bible as the literal word of God, and they brooked no

As an armed relative keeps watch from the farmhouse, a western Pennsylvania settler tends his livestock. The immigrant Calhouns made their first American home in this region, but the hostility of the weather, the Indians, and the French induced them to leave the area for western Virginia.

debate from their children. The basic education of Patrick and his siblings consisted of equal parts scripture, farming, and Indian fighting.

Hearing of newly opened lands to the west, the Calhouns decided to abandon Pennsylvania and its constant warfare. They farmed briefly in southwestern Virginia, then moved to the Long Canes region of northwestern South Carolina, where they lived from 1756 on. Patrick was 28 years old and a widower by the time his clan settled in South Carolina.

Part of the Carolina Piedmont, or "up-country," Long Canes featured great stands of timber alternating, noted one settler, with "an extended tract of prairie country, waving under a rich growth of cane, from 5 to 30 feet in height." When the Calhouns arrived, the area's residents included countless buffalo, some 20 other whites, and a large band of Cherokees. Patrick founded his farm about eight miles southwest of the modern town of Abbeville, on land the Cherokees had just ceded to South Carolina's colonial government.

In February 1760, the Cherokees attacked the Long Canes settlers; the raid's 50 victims included Patrick Calhoun's mother and older brother. Some settlers evacuated the region after the massacre, but not Patrick; refusing to give up his farm, he became a leader of the volunteer rangers who patrolled the Carolina-Georgia border, seeking out and battling the Cherokees. Finally, in 1764, Indians and whites signed a peace treaty.

Patrick Calhoun fought not only Indians but politicians; young John, who was one day to join their ranks, learned much from watching and listening to his father. Not very many years before John's birth, Patrick told him, the up-country might as well have been on the moon. Although about half of South Carolina's residents lived in the west, the region had no vote, no courts, no schools, no roads, no government protection against Indians and outlaws. The government in Charleston, almost 200 miles away on the seacoast, seemed unaware of the up-country's existence.

In 1769, Patrick appeared before the colonial legislature and made a plea for up-country courts, roads, and representation. The lawmakers turned a deaf ear. Patrick decided he would no longer tolerate such an attitude. A few months later, he enlisted a band of his coonskin-hatted neighbors and marched them 175 miles east, to the polling place near Charleston. Armed, angry, and not about to back off, the frontiersmen seized ballots and cast their votes—for Patrick Calhoun as their district's legislator. From that point on, the South Carolina frontier was politically represented.

A year after his descent on Charleston, 42-year-old, twice-widowed Patrick Calhoun married for the third time. Historians have discovered frustratingly little about the former Martha Caldwell, but she was said by her contemporaries to be "a great manager," a woman who had a flair for business and a knack for running a plantation. Described as "tall," "stately," and "cultured," Martha Calhoun was also portrayed as a "dark Irish beauty."

Over the next 15 years, Martha and Patrick would become the parents of five children: William, James, and Catherine were born before John's birth in 1782; the couple's last child, Patrick, Jr., arrived a few years later. As his family grew, Patrick, Sr., continued his political activities. Almost 50 years old at the outbreak of the American Revolution in 1775, he did not serve in the revolutionary forces, but he did represent his district in the South Carolina congresses that declared the colony's independence from Great Britain. Afterward, he returned to Long Canes to protect his family and farm—by now a large and prosperous plantation—against the British Army, their Indian allies, and local royalist guerrillas.

Patrick Calhoun had steadily increased his holdings; by the time of John's birth, he was among the up-country's wealthiest farmers. His family lived in a fine two-story, eight-room frame house, the first such building in the district. A census taken in 1790, when John was eight years old, showed that his father owned 31 black slaves, making him

Indians ambush colonial soldiers in Virginia in 1755. Enduring even heavier Indian attacks here than they had in Pennsylvania, the Calhoun family moved to the South Carolina hills in 1756. Two years later, Cherokees massacred Patrick Calhoun's mother and brother, but the young man stayed in the "up-country," where he eventually carved out a plantation, acquired slaves, married for the third time, and, in 1782, became the father of John C. Calhoun.

the second largest slaveholder in the entire South Carolina Piedmont.

Despite their prosperity, the Calhouns could not match the wealthy, easy-living aristocrats of the South Carolina coast. Vast lowland holdings planted with rice or cotton and worked by armies of slaves brought almost unimaginable wealth to these planters, who built luxurious mansions in the country and opulent townhouses in Charleston. In the Calhoun fields, everyone—black and white—worked together. As he grew older, John helped his father, his brothers, and the slaves as they tended the family's acres of corn, wheat, and oats and herds of cattle, sheep, and pigs.

As a boy, John learned history and political philosophy from his highly opinionated father. The less government, the better, said the self-made frontier planter. Never trust lawyers, never trust Indians or easterners. In fact, said Patrick Calhoun to his son, never trust anybody but yourself and then only after a careful review and analysis of all known facts. Indebt yourself to no one, Patrick ordered, and fight for what you believe in. As Calhoun biographer Margaret L. Coit has noted, "The sturdy old pioneer left his boy a rugged, typically American heritage." John would never forget his father's counsel.

Patrick Calhoun bitterly opposed South Carolina's ratification of the federal Constitution of 1787, and his son John later explained why: the document "permitted people other than those of South Carolina to tax the people of South Carolina, and thus allowed taxation without representation, which was a violation of the fundamental principle of the revolutionary struggle." Patrick finally accepted the Constitution, but only after the 10 amendments known as the Bill of Rights were added. As he saw it, the amendments protected the liberties of individuals and local governments from the power of the distant federal government. Here were more ideas John Calhoun would remember all his life.

John gained deep insights from his father's teachings, but he received little formal education in his early years. At the age of eight, he attended a back-country schoolhouse for a few months, but he learned only to read and write his name and to add simple figures. Except for that class, the area offered no school of any kind, not even an occasional church whose minister might teach frontier children basic reading and mathematics. And books were almost nonexistent on the frontier.

As for religion, the Calhoun children learned it largely from their mother, who taught them biblical history and Christian morality. Whenever a frontier circuit rider (traveling preacher) held services in their area, the Calhouns attended, but most of their devotions were led by Patrick, reading from the huge old family Bible on Sunday mornings.

In late 1795, John's sister married Moses Waddel, a clergyman and schoolmaster from Appling, Georgia. The young couple invited 13-year-old John to live with them in Appling, some 50 miles from Abbeville, and to attend Waddel's school there. John's parents gave their blessing, and he headed south with high hopes. Within two months of his arrival, however, sister Catherine suddenly sickened and died. The grief-stricken Waddel closed his school and set out on a round of circuit preaching, leaving John almost entirely alone for two months.

The boy dealt with his own sorrow by burying himself in Waddel's books. Most of them, predictably, dealt with theology, but the minister also enjoyed history, and John soon discovered that he did, too. John became so involved in his books that he slept little, rarely exercised or even went outside, and often skipped meals. In February 1796, when Waddel returned and found his young brother-in-law thin, pale, and red of eye, he sent him home at once. News traveled slowly in the up-country; not until John reached the family farm did he learn the shocking news about his father: Patrick Calhoun, 68, had died of lung disease two weeks earlier. The stunned youth learned that his two older brothers had left the farm to try their hand at business, James in Charleston, William in Augusta, Georgia. Instead of the active, noisy

When clergyman-school-master Moses Waddel married Catherine Calhoun in 1795, the couple invited the bride's brother John to live with them. The plan delighted the 13-year-old boy, but two months after he moved in, Catherine suddenly died, the grieving Moses went off on a preaching trip, and John found himself with no company but Waddel's books—which he proceeded to devour.

household of his youth, then, John found a sad, quiet residence inhabited only by his mother and his younger brother, Patrick.

Advised by his frugal and levelheaded mother, John gradually took over the management of his father's property. For the next five years, he tended livestock and cultivated cotton, working from first light to last—and finding deep satisfaction in it. As an adult, John Calhoun often remarked that he had never been as happy as when he worked his own farm. The land, observes biographer Coit, was "part of [Calhoun's] emotional and physical being. Everything that he said or did in later life can be traced back to this love and understanding of the earth from which he sprang."

Following the practice of his father, Calhoun worked side by side with his slaves. Years later, Sawney, his boyhood companion and personal servant, proudly told an interviewer, "We worked in the field, and many's the times in the [broiling] sun me and Marse John has plowed together." But despite his close and regular contact with the slaves, John Calhoun unquestioningly accepted the belief—common in the pre–Civil War South—that blacks were morally and mentally inferior to their white masters.

At this stage of his life, Calhoun's ambitions were limited: he wanted to take care of his mother, to prosper as a planter, and, in his rare free hours, to go hunting or fishing with Sawney. Although he also loved to read, he spent little time with books for the simple reason that he had none. But whatever he could find to read, he read. Having somehow obtained a copy of the South Carolina *Gazette*, he treated it as a rare treasure. The well-worn newspaper, dated May 10, 1798, still exists, its important articles carefully underlined in pencil by the young farmer. When a book did make its way up to the Piedmont and into his hands, Calhoun never let it out of his sight. A farmer who lived in the area once reported spotting John plowing a field and whistling happily, his eyes glued to a book he had tied to the plow handle.

Recognizing her son's unusual intelligence, Martha Calhoun asked James and William to come home and discuss education with him. When they broached the subject, however, John turned a cold shoulder: he would not consider leaving the farm or his mother to go to school. But, said the brothers, she wanted him to, and furthermore, Moses Waddel's academy in Appling was back in business. John finally said that as his family truly wished it, he would seek an education, but only on certain conditions: he wanted the best schooling available or none at all. Would his brothers be willing to finance seven years of study at the schools of his choice? They would, they replied.

In June 1800, 18-year-old John Calhoun left for Georgia to attend Waddel's revived academy. He cut a distinctive figure, with his stiff brown hair standing straight up on his head, his thin, strong, six-foot-two-inch frame giving him an angular appearance, and his square jaw, deep-set eyes, and heavy brows reflecting his intense, unusually serious nature.

Life at Waddel's school demanded the sort of health and strength that John had developed on the farm. He and his fellow students lived in log cabins in the woods, ate corn bread and bacon three times a day, rose at dawn for group prayers, and studied by the light of pine torches. Because the two-room log schoolhouse had no chairs, they spent their long school days on their feet, listening to Waddel and reciting their lessons in Latin, Greek, mathematics, moral philosophy, and debate.

Martha Calhoun died in her son's second year at the academy. The shock added to the feelings of loss and insecurity Calhoun had experienced after losing his sister and his father, but he forced himself to continue on his own, and redoubled his efforts at school. His work paid off. After two years of intense training under Waddel's eye, he qualified to enter the junior class at one of the nation's finest educational institutions: Yale College in New Haven, Connecticut.

By the age of 20, John Calhoun had lost some of his adolescent awkwardness, but his wiry brown hair still refused to lie down, and his six-foot-two-inch frame remained lean and angular. Although he was unusually solemn for a college freshman, the South Carolinian did form a few close friendships at Yale College, which he entered in 1802.

3

A Frontiersman at Yale

CALHOUN MADE THE 800-MILE JOURNEY from Abbeville to New Haven in the fall of 1802. With its 4,000 inhabitants, bustling wharves, and crisply carpentered houses, the Connecticut shore town represented a new—and exhilarating—world for the 20-year-old frontier farmer. Yale boasted an array of handsome, five-story brick buildings, crowned with cupolas and stretching for an entire block along College Street. Across the way, two brick churches and the city's colonial statehouse framed the green, a large, grassy field where residents (and sometimes cows) strolled amid the trees.

Yale had recently expanded its curriculum under the direction of its president, Timothy Dwight. Students could choose from courses in English grammar, surveying, navigation, modern languages, chemistry, and geography in addition to the required Greek and Latin. The college preserved the classic moral sternness of New England: attendance at morning and evening chapel services was compulsory for all students, and any Yaleman who denied the Bible's "divine authority" was subject to immediate dismissal.

Yale's laws also forbade students to drink liquor, make bets, or attend the theater for "any comedy or tragedy," and stated that "If any Scholar shall go a-fishing or sailing . . . he may be fined not exceeding thirty cents." A man's college years, the laws stated firmly, were not to be regarded as a "season of recreation."

Calhoun's class included 65 other men, most of them northerners bound for the ministry. He liked the strictness of Yale's moral climate, which matched well with his own strict, Presbyterian upbringing, and, to his surprise, he soon discovered he had received a better education than many of his colleagues. In his first mathematics class, he nervously surveyed the other young men, most of them products of the nation's best preparatory schools, including the famed academies at Andover and Exeter. Then he quickly figured the answer to the professor's question and looked around. All the other students were frowning, scratching at their slates, searching for the answer. The teacher checked Calhoun's slate and told him his answer was correct.

Top-hatted Yalemen toss a ball around the college yard in 1807. Calhoun feared that his fellow students, most of them from first-rate New England preparatory schools, would be miles ahead of him in learning, but the opposite proved true: educated in Moses Waddel's "backwoods" school, the young southerner found himself better prepared than most of his peers.

This sequence was repeated; in class after class, the first student to solve problems turned out to be Calhoun, a circumstance that, he said later, "gratified" him. As the year went on, his confidence increased. His studies proved, as he wrote a friend, "pleasant, and not very difficult," and he soon gained recognition as a "brilliant" student, especially in courses listed as "metaphysics, mathematics, and the precise sciences." The young man from the Carolina up-country was on his way.

Despite his reserved nature, Calhoun made some close friends, New Englanders as well as young men from his own state. He said he found Yankees "more penurious, more contracted in their sentiments, and less social, than the Carolinians," but he also considered them more virtuous. "As to morality," he conceded, the southerners "must yield" to the New Englanders. During his first year at Yale, he won election to the Phi Beta Kappa fraternity, at the time a social fraternity as well as a fellowship of the brightest students.

Despite his general acceptance by his peers, Calhoun did face a certain amount of snobbishness at Yale. Writing to a cousin, he commented that "[there exists] a considerable prejudice here against both the southern states and students." Some of the rich Carolina planters' sons, too, looked down their noses at the up-country farmer.

Calhoun's politics also set him apart. During the early 1800s, most Yale faculty members and students were Federalists, believing in a strong national government and favoring the interests of merchants over those of farmers. Staunch Federalists regarded Democratic Republican Thomas Jefferson's 1800 election to the presidency as a disaster; an idealistic gentleman farmer, Jefferson insisted that any government belonged to its citizens, a concept that naturally horrified Federalists. When Jefferson's Louisiana Purchase of 1803 appeared likely to create new states, thus ending New England's domination of national politics, some of the region's Federalists even muttered darkly about seceding from the Union.

Born and bred a Jeffersonian republican, Patrick Calhoun's son never pretended to respect Federalism in any form, a position that naturally made him a heretic at Yale. In 1804, his senior year, he attended a moral philosophy class taught by President Dwight—an almost fanatical Federalist—himself. One day, after heaping glory on Federalism and denouncing as "vicious" the Jeffersonian doctrine of sovereignty of the people, Dwight asked the class a question: "What is the legitimate source of power?" Jutting out his formidable chin, Calhoun rose to his full height and answered. "The people," he said.

Dwight almost exploded. Then, getting a grip on himself, he began a debate with this young southern upstart. As the rest of the class looked on in silent awe, Calhoun and Dwight battled it out for the rest of the afternoon, neither man giving an inch, each defending his position with force, wit, and logic. The argument ended in a draw—and in Dwight's grudging respect for this unconventional frontiersman. "Young man," he said at last, "your talents are of a high order and might justify you for any station, but I deeply regret that you do not love sound principles. . . . You seem to possess a most unfortunate bias for error."

That evening, speaking privately to a friend (who "privately" repeated his words to other friends), Dwight said young Calhoun might have the ability "to be president of the United States"; he would not "be surprised," the college chief admitted, "to see him one day occupy that office."

Naturally, someone finally told Calhoun about Dwight's remarks. What he thought will never be known, but perhaps it was then that he first considered a career in politics. In any case, from that point on, when fellow students teased him for being a "grind," working when everyone else was relaxing, Calhoun had a stock response. He said he studied hard, one classmate later recalled, "in order that he might acquit himself creditably when he should become a member of Congress!" Another friend recalled Calhoun saying, "I would leave college this very day if I doubted my ability to reach Congress within three years."

Like his father, John Calhoun loved a good argument; night after night until dawn, he sat up debating politics, religion, and philosophical questions with his friends. But on one subject—the opposite sex—Calhoun had no comments. Although he was said to have a "special liking" for a local beauty, 20-year-old Sarah Sherman, he limited his courtship to sedate daylight strolls and family tea parties, and he never spoke of her to others.

His personal discretion and unorthodox political views amused his friends. One of them, 25-year-old Ben Silliman of Connecticut called the 22-year-old Calhoun "a first-rate young man . . . for pure and gentlemanly conduct," but added that "his mind was of a peculiar structure, and his views also were often peculiar." Calhoun's mixture of propriety and political ambition became something of a legend, inspiring a humorous song, "Calhoun, My Jo" (*Jo* is a Scottish word meaning "dear" or "sweetheart"):

> John C. Calhoun, my Jo, John,
> When first we were acquaint
> You were my chum at Yale, John—
> And something of a saint.
> And Dr. Dwight, God bless him, John,
> Predicted as you know
> You'd be the Nation's President,
> John C. Calhoun, my Jo.

For his senior oration, Calhoun wrote a speech entitled "The Qualifications Necessary to Constitute an Ideal Statesman." Unfortunately, he never delivered it; a month before graduation, he was laid low with a serious illness, which some modern biographers suspect was yellow fever. Although, as he regretfully put it, he could take no part in "either the pleasures or the exercises of the day," he graduated with high honors, a distinction that confirmed his unshakable confidence in his own intelligence and abilities.

While he was recovering from his illness, Calhoun received a letter from Floride Bonneau Colhoun, the wealthy widow of his cousin, Senator John Ewing Colhoun who

When the widowed Floride Colhoun (the member of a family branch that retained the name's Scottish spelling), learned that cousin John Calhoun was ill in 1804, she invited him to visit her in Newport, Rhode Island. The mother of two boys and a girl, the wealthy and attractive socialite adored the tall, charming Yale student, whom she soon began treating as one of her own sons.

had preserved the Scottish spelling of the family name). Mrs. Colhoun, who was spending the summer with her three children in Newport, Rhode Island, had heard of her cousin-in-law's illness and wanted him to come and convalesce at her summer home. She had never met John, but she was a cousin and a southerner, and southerners "did for" their kin. Calhoun accepted with pleasure.

Arriving in Newport in September 1804, he met Cousin Floride, a handsome, dark-haired woman some 12 years his senior; her sons, John Ewing, 13, and James Edward, 6; and her daughter, 12-year-old Floride Bonneau. His relatives gave Calhoun a sense of family security he had not felt since leaving Long Canes, and he thoroughly enjoyed their company. Sometimes rather starchy in social situations, he displayed an easy and captivating charm with children, whom he genuinely liked.

The youngsters adored Cousin John, and so did their mother, who soon began treating him as an adopted son. She introduced him to her friends, giving him his first contact with the aristocrats of the Carolina shoreline, and she insisted he come along when she took her family on a pleasure trip to Boston that summer; she also asked him to travel back to Charleston with her family.

Calhoun returned the affection of his "stepmother"; family legend maintains that he even fell in love with her. Whether he did or not, the relationship benefited both sides. Floride Colhoun's intimacy with the tidewater elite would prove extremely important to a budding politician; in turn, she seemed to enjoy displaying her tall, intense young protégé to her fashionable friends and acquaintances.

The best route to politics, Calhoun decided, would be a legal career. Accordingly, in the fall of 1804, he returned to Charleston with Floride Colhoun, who had found him a place in the office of Judge William Henry De Saussure, her own attorney and one of the leading lawyers in South Carolina. Calhoun impressed De Saussure, who told friends he thought the young man had both "a superior mind" and "more knowledge than is usual at his age."

Many law students of the time educated themselves by studying with an established lawyer and then learning as they went along. But Calhoun never did anything halfway: if he was to be a lawyer, he would go to law school—and not just any law school, but the nation's finest. He applied to, and was accepted at, the celebrated academy of law run by Judge Tapping Reeve in Litchfield, Connecticut.

In the spring of 1805, Calhoun once again headed north. Family records indicate that he paused in Charlottesville, Virginia, on the way. Not all historians agree that he made the stopover, but according to some, he halted his carriage at the edge of a magnificent estate. It was Monticello, an extraordinary, classically inspired mansion set in a sweep of meticulously landscaped lawns. Its owner was Thomas Jefferson, president of the United States.

"There is no greater proof of the simplicity of American democracy in those early days," notes biographer Margaret Coit, "than an unknown young frontier American walking up to the door of Monticello, seeking and winning an audience with the president." No official record of this meeting exists, but the 23-year-old law student's political ideas might have intrigued the 62-year-old Jefferson. He usually retired each night at nine, but on the night of Calhoun's visit, he is said to have stayed up talking until well after midnight, then insisted that his caller spend the night and join him for more talk at breakfast.

Those conversations may have ignited the men's friendship, which unquestionably continued for the next 20 years. At Monticello, they would have discussed their similarities—both were strong anti-Federalists, slaveholders, and planters; both believed the nation's future lay with its farmland rather than its cities; both believed that the states, not the federal government, should deal with such questions as slavery. Whatever they said, their visit would have forged a link between two generations of democracy: the passing of the Jeffersonian torch from the great man who lighted it to the fiery youth who would carry it forward.

Household workers—probably slaves—sweep the walk at Monticello, Thomas Jefferson's magnificent home near Charlottesville, Virginia. One day in 1805, according to Calhoun family records, a stranger—23-year-old John Calhoun—marched up this same walk, knocked on the door, received a warm welcome, and wound up talking politics with the 62-year-old U.S. president far into the night.

Calhoun's stern Presbyterianism made some people at Yale regard him as too "proper," inhibited to the point of prudishness. At law school in ultraconservative Litchfield, Connecticut, however, Calhoun was seen as a flaming liberal, a potentially dangerous man who resembled Thomas Jefferson and his band of "atheists and libertines."

4

From Law to Politics

IN JULY 1805, A STAGECOACH clanked to a stop in the center of Litchfield. Jumping from the vehicle, John Calhoun stretched his long legs and took a look around the western Connecticut village where he would spend the next two years. He saw four main streets intersecting at the green, where a whipping post silently reminded citizens to honor the Sabbath; he also saw a church, a schoolhouse, an inn, and a number of handsome houses, one of which belonged to Judge Tapping Reeve. Behind the judge's stately two-story home stood a tiny one-room structure: the celebrated law school at which Calhoun would finish his education.

Six mornings a week, Calhoun would soon learn, some two dozen students crowded into the little house to listen to lectures by Reeve or his assistant, James Gould. In the afternoons, the students studied philosophy, history, and literature. Once a week they held mock trials to practice arguing cases before the bench.

Tall, craggy-faced, and unconventional, the 65-year-old Reeve wore his gray hair long, dressed in the knee breeches and stockings of a bygone era, and spoke in choppy, sometimes confusing sentences. He was politically conservative, brilliant, and controversial—some people were outraged by his strong support for women's rights—but his quick wit and generous nature had endeared him to generations of law students. Calhoun was no exception; he felt "particularly fortunate," he told his cousin Floride, to be studying with the distinguished judge, and to be treated by him in such a surprisingly "open and agreeable" manner.

Reeve's colleague, 35-year-old James Gould, lacked the quirky genius of his mentor, but he proved a crisp and effective instructor. He insisted that his students organize their thoughts logically, prepare thoroughly before an argument, and, in debates, rely on their memories instead of notes. From Gould, Calhoun learned the techniques of logical analysis and unrehearsed speaking that would become

In this small, single-room building, Calhoun learned the fundamentals of law that he would depend on all his life. The South Carolina law student lived in a house near the school, where for $47 per year he got a large, airy room and a substantial daily dinner of beef, potatoes, bread, and cabbage.

his hallmarks. From Reeve, he learned the law, its spirit as well as its letter. As one of Calhoun's fellow students put it, students finished their time with Judge Reeve determined to be "the defenders of the right and the avengers of the wrong."

From both professors, Calhoun learned the tactics of ideological war: as a Jeffersonian republican, the South Carolinian found himself part of a tiny, embattled minority. Here in Litchfield, faculty, students, and townspeople were solidly Federalist, solidly anti-Jefferson, their beliefs the total opposite of Calhoun's. (In 1799, Reeve had predicted that if Jefferson was elected, the nation's streets would run with blood. He had even managed to get himself indicted by a federal grand jury for libeling the president in a newspaper article, although at Jefferson's specific request the government dropped the charges.)

Outspoken as ever, Calhoun made no secret of his political convictions, and his passionate support of Jefferson and republicanism drew dark looks from the ultraconservative New England community. "This place is so much agitated by party feelings," Calhoun confided to his cousin, "that [I] find it prudent to form few connections in town. . . . I take little amusement and live a very studious life."

The young southerner, in other words, received almost no invitations to Litchfield's social events. Everywhere he went, he felt critical or curious eyes fixed on him. But, he said—somewhat unconvincingly—being left out had its benefits; time spent by himself was "not unfavorable" to his studies. And he did enjoy the disciplined study and practice debates. "No period of my life," he wrote later, "has been spent more advantageously to myself."

Calhoun's legal education at Litchfield prepared him for the political career he would pursue. Even better preparation for his particular future, however, was Reeve's passionate opposition to the Jeffersonian democracy that Calhoun honored so deeply. It was at the judge's academy that Calhoun first heard intelligent, articulate people discuss

Judge Tapping Reeve glances up from his papers at America's first legal academy, Litchfield Law School, which he founded in 1784. Calhoun's teacher was a classic "absent-minded professor," but beneath his eccentric manner lay a brilliant mind, often far ahead of its time. Reeve believed, for example, in women's rights, asserting that "the fairer sex" had not only rights but "most happily for [men]," wills and ideas of their own.

secession. Reeve and his colleagues argued often and emphatically that, if Jefferson and his crew of "atheists and libertines" impinged on the rights of New England, then New England had not only the *moral* but the *legal* right to refuse to obey federal laws—an act called *nullification*—and to withdraw from the Union. Calhoun listened with interest.

In the fall of 1806, he finished law school and caught a stagecoach to Philadelphia. There, he bought a horse and headed for Charleston, where he would study with Judge De Saussure for a few months. After that, he hoped to open his own law practice and make a lot of money quickly, then abandon his legal career, buy a plantation, and enter politics.

Meanwhile, Calhoun had to live in rollicking, high-spirited Charleston, and he liked it not at all. New Englanders had assumed that because he was "free in his conversation," he was probably freethinking in religion, but they were mistaken. Even as a young man, Calhoun was traditional, solidly wedded to the stern Presbyterian morality of his forebears. He considered Charleston society, with its balls, theaters, and ostentatious wealth, blasphemous and "extremely corrupt"; he even went so far as to describe an outbreak of deadly yellow fever as God's punishment for Charleston's "sins and debaucheries." Finally, after studying law with De Saussure for six months, Calhoun abandoned Charleston altogether.

Back in comfortingly familiar Abbeville, Calhoun served a brief apprenticeship with a local attorney, then took—and passed—the state bar examination (the test qualifying him to practice law in South Carolina). Converting an old, red-painted log cabin into an office, the 25-year-old attorney hung up his shingle and waited for clients. He did not have to wait long.

On the frontier, where hardship and risk were constant presences, Americans tended to live their lives at full speed. Not everyone, of course, belted down huge quantities of hard liquor, bet on cockfights and card games, swore lustily, or settled disputes with their fists, but many did. And many lawyers lived lives only slightly less riotous than their clients. But not John Calhoun. Straitlaced, solemn to the point of humorlessness, and given to cool, lucid courtroom speeches rather than the emotional appeals and flamboyant orations of his peers, he might have seemed a likely candidate for failure in the uninhibited up-country. In fact, he proved the exact opposite.

Perhaps it was Calhoun's very differences from the typical frontier lawyer that attracted people. Instead of thunderously exaggerating a client's innocence, he would bring articulate, finely honed legal arguments to the courtroom, expounding on precedents and "the wider field of natural justice." But despite his success, Calhoun never liked legal work—"I still feel a strong aversion to the law, and am determined to forsake it as soon as I can make a decent independence," he wrote Floride Colhoun—but he was indisputedly good at it. Standing out among the lawyers of the up-country, he soon had all the business he could handle, his practice extending beyond Abbeville and its neighboring counties as far east as the state's new capital city, Columbia.

Calhoun may have disliked the lawyer's profession, but he loved a good debate, and few men of his time could match him as a speechmaker. It was this gift, coupled with an act of British hostility, that catapulted him into politics in 1807.

Tensions between the United States and Great Britain had been steadily rising since 1805, when the British Navy had begun halting American vessels on the high seas and seizing sailors suspected of being British deserters. In June 1807, the British naval ship HMS *Leopard* stopped the *Chesapeake*, a frigate of the U.S. Navy, off Hampton Roads, Virginia. When the American skipper refused to allow a British inspection, the *Leopard* opened fire, killing or wounding 24 American sailors and forcing the unprepared *Chesapeake* to strike her colors. The British then boarded and seized four men.

Americans reacted to the attack with volcanic outrage. Across the young nation, townspeople gathered to denounce Britain and demand revenge for this blow to American honor. Abbeville's citizens, as furious as anyone in the country, decided to hold a mass protest meeting and send a series of resolutions to Congress. Given the honor of writing the resolutions and addressing the meeting was that promising up-country attorney, John C. Calhoun.

No aspiring politician could have asked for a better forum. Bursting with patriotism and rage, people from all over the Piedmont converged on Abbeville, where they listened with mounting excitement as the tall, craggy frontier lawyer addressed them. Not yet a polished orator, Calhoun made up for his lack of experience with sincere passion, denouncing the insults of foreigners, extolling the Stars and Stripes, and declaring the perfidious British lion no match for the bold American eagle. His listeners cheered themselves hoarse.

Calhoun's admirers did more than shout his praises: they elected him to the South Carolina state legislature. In the fall of 1808, he traveled to Columbia and took the seat once occupied by his father. Fiery, deeply committed, and unshakeably confident in his own views, the 26-year-old Calhoun quickly caught the attention of the older politicians in the legislature. Soon after Calhoun's arrival in Columbia, the Speaker of the House, Joseph Alston, approached the Democratic Republicans' elder statesman, Daniel Huger, about the new member. According to Huger's recollections, Alston said, "I'm afraid that I shall find this long, gawky fellow from Abbeville hard to manage." He was right.

Outspoken and sometimes lacking in tact, Calhoun stirred resentment among some of his fellow lawmakers, once nearly provoking a duel. But his intelligence and determined views—that South Carolina take a major role in national affairs, and that the country must prepare for an inevitable war with Great Britain—began to attract confidence, and soon made him principal spokesman for the legislature's anti-British Democratic Republicans. In the near future, Calhoun's legislative performance would bring him even broader political power.

Meanwhile, his interests began to take a new direction. Over the years, he had remained close to his cousin Floride and her family, but in the spring of 1808, he had made an interesting discovery: his cousin's daughter, also named Floride, was now 16 years old. She had blossomed into a classic southern belle—graceful, lovely to look at, flirtatious, and strong-willed. Visiting his cousins' coastal plantation, Bonneau's Ferry, the following Christmas, Calhoun made another discovery: he was in love. The event shocked him. "I formerly thought," he wrote in his characteristically stiff and formal style, "that it would be impossible for me to be strongly agitated in an affair of this kind, but that opinion now seems to me to be totally unfounded."

Calhoun's wish to marry young Floride delighted her mother, but the teenager was in no hurry to give up her carefree life as the belle of Charleston. Calhoun resigned himself to waiting, but in the meantime, he showered his potential mother-in-law with nervous letters. "It will be useless for me to conceal from you my increased anxiety on [the subject of marriage]," he said in one missive. "The more I reflect on it, the more indissolubly does my happiness seem to be connected with that event. If I should be disappointed by any adverse circumstance . . . it will be by far the most unlucky incident in my life."

"Madly in love," as he put it, Calhoun even tried writing poetry—an almost impossible task for so reserved and lawyerlike a man. He finally managed to compose one love poem, but it may have failed to excite Floride: every line started with "whereas" except the last, which began with "wherefore." Calhoun's single surviving love letter betrays passionate feelings, but his language is wooden even for 1810. ("To be united in mutual virtuous love," reads one of the warmer passages, "is the first and best bliss that God has permitted to our natures.")

Clumsy or not, Calhoun won his lady's heart; in the spring of 1810, she promised to marry him the following winter. Elated, he rode off in search of a plantation where he could settle with his bride; he found what he wanted, an 800-acre estate called Bath, in Willington, South Carolina, not far from his original home in Abbeville. Calhoun's engagement not only filled him with joy, it also helped his career. To succeed in South Carolina politics, a candidate needed the blessing of the tidewater aristocrats as well as support in the up-country; Calhoun already had the latter, and marriage into the Bonneau clan made certain he would have the rest.

In 1810, Calhoun received the Democratic Republican nomination for U.S. congressman from the Abbeville-

Floride Bonneau Colhoun married her distant cousin John Calhoun on January 8, 1811. The ceremony, held at Bonneau's Ferry, brought John's brothers and friends from the Piedmont and Floride's "kissing kin" from Charleston and the Low Country. "It was a grand affair, that wedding," recalled Floride's younger brother, James, "an old-time wedding; everybody was there."

Laurens-Newberry district. He campaigned vigorously, emphasizing the still-smoldering national anger about the *Chesapeake* incident, and talking of war with England. He and the party managers felt confident of his victory, but no one expected the actual event: a voting landslide that buried the Federalist candidate in November 1810.

Two months later, John and Floride married in a lavish ceremony at Bonneau's Ferry. After the wedding, they visited their unfinished home at Bath, then spent the rest of the winter in Charleston. By spring, Floride Calhoun realized she was pregnant; she and her husband returned to Bonneau's Ferry. Leaving her with her mother, Calhoun rode around the state winding up his law practice.

On October 15, Floride Calhoun gave birth to a son, whom the couple named Andrew Pickens, after a Revolutionary War–hero relative. Calhoun waited at Bonneau's Ferry until he was sure his wife and son were doing well, then set off for Washington, D.C., to take his seat in the United States Congress.

*Artist Rembrandt Peale sketched this likeness of Calhoun soon after
the new congressman arrived in Washington, D.C., in 1811. Calhoun,
perceived as too prim at Yale and too radical at Litchfield, was judged
just right by Washington's old hands: "He is well informed, easy in
his manners and . . . admirable in his disposition," observed one
admiring colleague.*

5

The Young Hercules

WASHINGTON, D.C., WAS LITTLE more than an overgrown village when Calhoun arrived there in the fall of 1811. A 10-mile-square of Virginia and Maryland wilderness selected by the nation's first president (and the city's namesake), the capital had begun to take shape in 1800. A decade later, elegant homes and stately government buildings, most of them still unfinished, alternated with swampland and vacant lots.

Radiating across the capital city was a network of broad but unpaved avenues, dusty in the summer, muddy the rest of the year. The Capitol itself, described by a local wit as "two wings without a body," so far consisted only of the Senate and the House chambers, connected by a wooden walkway. But what made Washington unique was not streets or buildings; it was an aura. No one lived here without some connection, weak or strong, direct or otherwise, to politics. The air virtually smelled of it. Calhoun took to it at once.

In 1811, the Capitol (viewed here from Pennsylvania Avenue) was an awkward structure—"two wings without a body," in the words of one observer— consisting of the House of Representatives and the Senate, linked by an open corridor. Like his fellow congressmen, Calhoun earned $6 per day and lived in a shared room in a dingy boardinghouse near the Capitol.

The South Carolinian's reputation as a promising politician had preceded him, and his new colleagues gave him a warm welcome. His first mentor was Speaker of the House Henry Clay, a lean, handsome Kentuckian, at 34 already the nation's second (after President James Madison) most influential man. Clay's inner circle was made up of congressmen from the new states in the West or the frontier regions of the old South. Most of them young, fiery, and eager for action, these politicians were known as War Hawks, a name given them by maverick Democratic Republican John ("Mad Jack") Randolph of Virginia.

The Hawks believed that America's honor demanded war. They wanted to drive the British out of Canada, and they wanted to end British support of the hostile Indians who endangered America's westward expansion. Last but not least, they wanted a halt to Britain's high-handed treatment of American shipping. "Free Trade and Sailors' Rights!" cried the War Hawks, insisting that war was necessary not only to rid North America of the British but to safeguard the nation's independence.

Recognizing Calhoun as a potential ally, Clay invited him to move into the boardinghouse where he and several like-minded congressmen lived. Calhoun soon felt at ease with his new colleagues, and they with him. "He is well informed, easy in his manners and I think admirable in his disposition," noted one southern congressman of the newcomer.

Speaker of the House Henry Clay, 35 years old, first met the 29-year-old Calhoun in 1811. The two men differed on many issues, including slavery, but they felt the same way about England: tired of seeing their nation "eternally tied to Britain's kite," they demanded— and, in 1812, obtained—a declaration of war.

Speaker Clay maintained power by placing his friends on crucial congressional committees. Soon deciding he had been right about Calhoun's value as a supporter, Clay assigned him to the House Foreign Relations Committee, where the South Carolinian quickly made his mark. He did this by conducting a verbal duel with the legendary —and notorious—Mad Jack Randolph, wielder of the sharpest tongue in Washington.

When the Foreign Relations Committee produced a prowar report, Randolph railed against the War Hawks' "agrarian cupidity"—their alleged greed for more farmland in the West—and accused them of promoting "empty patriotism." Referring to the Hawks' battle cry, "On to

Virginia's John ("Mad Jack") Randolph, surely one of the oddest characters in congressional history, was a dazzling orator, a bitter opponent of the War of 1812, and a master of scathing insult. Speaking of a fellow representative who disagreed with him, Randolph said, "He is a man of splendid abilities, but utterly corrupt. He shines and stinks like a rotten mackerel by moonlight."

Canada!," Randolph mockingly imitated the call of the whippoorwill (wip-per-WILL! wip-per-WILL!) and said the War Hawks had "but one monotonous tone—CanaDA! CanaDA! CanaDA!" As he concluded his tirade, Randolph shook his long, bony finger at the War Hawks. "You sign your political death warrant!" he shouted.

Calhoun, making his first important speech before the House, replied to Randolph two days later, on December 13, 1811. Speaking without notes but with great precision, he began by answering Randolph's "death warrant" taunt: "The honor of a nation is its life," he declared. "Deliberately to abandon it is to commit an act of political suicide." After asserting that only a government willing to defend its citizens' freedom and interests could maintain the Union, Calhoun's face darkened, his voice rose, and he fixed his eyes directly on Randolph. "A sense of independence and honor," he thundered, is "so imposing as to enforce silence upon even the gentleman from Virginia!"

As Calhoun took his seat, colleagues swarmed around him, reaching fo his hand, clapping his shoulder, and loudly congratulating him. Even his opponents felt grudging admiration for this brash young man from the frontier who had dared to lock horns with the mighty Jack Randolph. Newspapers across the land reported his speech, for the most part favorably. The Richmond *Enquirer*, for example, predicted that Calhoun would surely become "one of those master-spirits, who stamp their names upon the age which they live."

Calhoun cooperated closely with Clay in pushing the Congress and the president toward war. The War Hawks faced tough opposition from the Federalists, who argued that Americans had no unsolvable quarrel with England, and that the United States was ill-prepared to fight the powerful British navy. The Federalists, however, were no match for the determined, well-organized War Hawks. In June 1812, Calhoun—by now chairman of the Foreign Relations Com-mittee—presented the House with a war resolution; both

The Hartford Convention or *LEAP NO LEAP.*

A cartoon mocks the states that considered secession during the War of 1812. As England's King George III shouts, "O 'tis my Yankey boys! Jump in, my fine fellows," Massachusetts (top right) says, "What a dangerous leap!!! but we must jump, Brother Conn." Connecticut says, "Little Rhode will jump the first," but Rhode Island wails, "Poor little I, what will become of me? This leap is of a frightful size."

houses of Congress passed it, and on June 18, President Madison signed it. The United States, for the second time in its brief existence, was at war.

America was divided over the War of 1812. The West and the South had wanted it passionately; Northeasterners, fearing loss of the trade they depended upon, had opposed it with equal fervor. New England greeted the war's reality with a mournful tolling of churchbells, but elsewhere, jubilant citizens fired their rifles and raised their glasses. South Carolinians, who expected the war to bring them more land and fewer Indians, cheered loud and long for their representative, who, along with Clay, could take most of the responsibility for this war.

Calhoun himself was not only exultant, but highly optimistic. In four weeks' time from the declaration, he maintained, "Canada will be in our power." The war, he assured the public, would teach the world that Americans had inherited not only their liberty "but also the will and the power to maintain it."

But under his triumph, Calhoun was lonely; he keenly missed Floride and Andrew, the boy he still hardly knew. He had dreamed "all night last night," he wrote his wife, "of being home with you; and nursing our dear son; and regretted when I awoke to find it a dream." Writing to his mother-in-law, he said he had "nothing to render me uneasy but my solicitude for those I have left behind." Washington was "quite gay," but, he noted forlornly, "I do not participate in it much myself."

Calhoun's confidence about the War of 1812, at least at the beginning, was sadly misplaced. The War Hawks had relied on manpower superiority—the United States had seven and one-quarter million people to British Canada's half-million—without stopping to count U.S. troops: there were only 2,765 men under arms, including officers. The U.S. Navy, furthermore, boasted exactly 15 ships of war, compared to the British Royal Navy's 75 ships of the line. At first, however, none of these details worried the War Hawks. On to Canada!

At the war's outset, everything went wrong. Massachusetts and Connecticut refused to supply troops for what they called "Mr. Madison's War," and New Englanders once again spoke of secession. A three-pronged invasion of Canada failed miserably; Detroit surrendered without firing a shot; Chicago fell to a British-Indian force led by the great Shawnee warrior Tecumseh. Then the tide began to turn.

In September 1813, a young American naval captain, Oliver Hazard Perry, wiped out a British fleet on Lake Erie, and American privateers (government-authorized, armed civilian vessels) began to capture or sink one British merchant ship after another. A little earlier, the U.S. frigate *Constitution* ("Old Ironsides") had soundly thrashed the mighty HMS *Guerrière*, pride of the king's navy.

In Congress, meanwhile, the Federalists—led by Daniel Webster, a New Hampshireman with beetling black brows and a genius for oratory—did their best to embarrass the administration and obstruct the war. At one point, after defeating a bill that would have encouraged enlistments, Webster wrote himself a gleeful little note about the Democratic Republicans: "They are in a sad pickle," he said. "Who cares?"

On their side, the Democratic Republicans—spearheaded by Calhoun—struggled to justify the war and to raise money and men to fight it. In repeated clashes with Webster, Calhoun warned the Federalists that their "factious opposition" to the war would bring about "national ruin." Calhoun's vigorous defense of his cause deeply impressed his party; Treasury Secretary Alexander J. Dallas, for example, called him the "young Hercules who carried the war on his shoulders."

In August 1814, "Young Hercules" found himself carrying even more weight: the British attacked Washington, burning most of it (including the President's House) to the ground. But the next month, the "Dirty Shirts," as the British contemptuously labeled the carelessly uniformed Americans, turned back a large British invasion force at Fort McHenry, Maryland. (At the end of a nightlong British bombardment of the fort, a young American lawyer named Frances Scott Key saw that "by dawn's early light," the "star-spangled banner" still waved. Inspired by the sight, he wrote a poem that, more than 100 years later, became his country's national anthem.)

By late 1814, the war was about at a draw, with neither side having an advantage over the other. On Christmas Eve, they signed a peace treaty in Ghent, Belgium. (In the end, the treaty never mentioned the boarding of American ships by the British, but the practice was quietly discontinued after the war). News traveled slowly, and the war went on; the Americans, in fact, scored their greatest victory in January 1815, when General Andrew ("Old Hickory") Jackson won the Battle of New Orleans.

On January 8, a huge British army advanced on the Louisiana city, defended by Jackson and a ragtag collection of backwoods militia, Choctaw Indians, Creoles, free blacks, and French pirates. Britain had sent her best—a force of well-disciplined, battle-hardened veterans, commanded by the able Sir Edward Pakenham—but they proved no match for the deadly hail of Jackson's sharpshooters. The American band cheerfully played "Hail, Columbia!" as the redcoats retreated, leaving 700 dead, 1,400 wounded, and 500 other prisoners. Jackson's losses: 8 dead and 13 wounded.

After news of the battle and the peace treaty arrived, Congress adjourned in a celebratory mood. Elated by national developments, Calhoun also rejoiced at the chance to spend some time with his family: his wife, Floride; his three-year-old son, Andrew; and his blond, curly-haired daughter, baby Floride, who had arrived in January 1814.

A British newspaper showed the burning of Washington, D.C., with this self-congratulatory caption: "On August 24, 1814, when we burnt and destroyed their Dock Yard with a Frigate and a Sloop of War, Rope-walk, Arsenal, Senate House, President's Palace, War Office, Treasury and the Great Bridge. With the Flotilla, the public property destroyed amounted to thirty Million of Dollars."

But the visit, which began so happily, ended in sorrow: one April night, the Calhouns awoke to hear Floride crying. Sweeping up her small, feverish form, they sent a messenger racing for the doctor, but it was too late. By sunrise, the child was dead.

"Everything was done," wrote the grief-wracked Calhoun to his mother-in-law, "but in vain." The baby's death, he said, was "the heaviest calamity that has ever occurred to us . . . our dear child . . . so healthy, so cheerful . . . she is gone alas! from us forever; and has left nothing behind but our grief and tears." Calhoun spent the next six months trying to comfort his wife; by fall, she seemed resigned to his returning to his responsibilities in Washington. Calhoun resolved that Floride would raise no more babies in the wilderness; her next child, due that coming spring, would be born in Charleston, where a doctor could always be found quickly. He hated to board the northbound coastal steamer, but Floride promised to write him every day, and he finally tipped his hat and headed back to the capital.

The war's outcome, along with Jackson's late but stunning triumph, had triggered an explosion of patriotism and confidence among Americans. The Federalist party ended the war with a stigma of disloyalty from which it never recovered, but the Democratic Republicans were riding high. Calhoun had insisted that the United States could defeat Great Britain, and he had been right; after these victories, he crowed, no one could treat America "like an illegitimate child in the family of nations."

His prestige thus increased, the young South Carolinian now emerged as the acknowledged leader of the Democratic Republican majority in Congress and as the principal spokesman of the lower South. He also impressed his peers with his manners and appearance. Women admired his firm mouth and thick, unruly hair; men praised what one colleague called his "intense and vibrant personality." Calhoun was easy to talk to, unfailingly respectful to his seniors and superiors, gracious and unpatronizing to those beneath his rank.

If he had a major flaw as a public personality, it lay in his speechmaking; in his early career, even his admirers admitted that, despite his capacity for impassioned debate, most of Calhoun's speeches were a bore. He was perhaps "not eloquent," said one cautious congressional friend. Another called him a man of "great sensitivity but limited eloquence." In an era, and particularly a Congress, full of brilliant, fiery orators, Calhoun was all too aware of his own shortcomings, but he worked on improvement. One future day, an eminent journalist would define him as "the most elegant speaker who sits in the House."

For all the accolades, Calhoun had been shaken by the War of 1812; he felt personally responsible for pushing his country into a conflict it had come close to losing. Now, in the war's aftermath, he began to look at America's future security, and what he saw was another clash with Great Britain. Certain that America's growing overseas trade would eventually lead to trouble with the "Ruler of the Waves," Calhoun began to work with Clay and other Democratic Republicans to prepare America for the next conflict.

Calhoun's vision covered a number of fronts. It included an expanded army and navy, military academies in every state, and coastal forts to protect shipping. To help develop American industry and reduce America's vulnerability to a blockade, he advocated a tariff, or tax, on imported goods. Perhaps the highest item on Calhoun's list was one called "internal improvements." The congressman wanted the government to build a network of roads and canals connecting all points of the nation; such a system, he said, would speed the movement of troops and supplies and make the nation less dependent on maritime transportation. Finally, he strongly urged his fellow legislators to create a national bank.

This bank would be a private corporation chartered by the government and jointly owned by the state and individual citizens. Such an institution, as he saw it, would have two principal purposes: to supply credit to business and indus-

New Hampshire congressman Daniel Webster, elected in 1813 as a "peace candidate," missed no opportunity to frustrate the administration's war effort. There were times, noted one historian, when it was hard for government leaders "to decide whether they were carrying on a war against England or [against] . . . Daniel Webster."

try, and to issue dependable, gold-backed paper money in a nation that, so far, had never had any standard currency. Calhoun and his supporters believed that a national bank would promote financial soundness in the United States, not only by supplying the country with a trustworthy money supply, but by providing the government with a source of credit in wartime.

Calhoun's broad program, which Clay later labeled the "American System"—military expansion, academies, forts, roads, tariffs, a national bank—would expand both the powers and the expenses of the federal government. That goal made sense to Calhoun, who believed that the government was responsible both for ensuring the nation's overall welfare and for footing the bills. He also had an eye on his political future: by identifying himself with a program that would benefit all parts of the nation, he hoped to build support for a future presidential campaign.

In 1816, Calhoun managed to push through two of his pet bills: the first chartered a Bank of the United States, popularly known as BUS; the second imposed a tariff upon imports. Moving full-steam ahead, Calhoun next started rounding up votes for the so-called Bonus Bill, a project very dear to his heart. This legislation would allow the government to use profits from the BUS to build the transportation system in which Calhoun so passionately believed.

The Bonus Bill would make it possible to link the East Coast cities with the frontier, the Hudson River with the Great Lakes, Maine with Louisiana. In fighting for the bill, Calhoun had given the most powerful speech of his career to date. "The more strongly we are bound together, the more inseparable are our destinies," he had said. "Let us, then, bind the republic together with a perfect system of roads and canals. *Let us conquer space!*" The vote was close, but the bill squeaked through, 86 to 84.

But Calhoun's triumph was short-lived. As one of his last acts of office, President James Madison vetoed the Bonus Bill, which he had decided was unconstitutional. Calhoun, who knew what the veto would mean to his home state, tried to change Madison's mind, but to no avail. Next, he tried to organize an override of the veto, but he was unable to get the needed two-thirds of the House to vote his way. After that, things worked out just as Calhoun had guessed they would.

Wealthy northern states were, without aid from the federal government, soon to link New York with the Great Lakes via the 363-mile-long Erie Canal, and the western states would continue to use the mighty Mississippi River to transport their produce to market. The defeat of the Bonus Bill, however, was to prove a disaster for the South, which, without federal aid, never found the means to build its own much-needed system of fast, cheap transportation.

In 1817, former secretary of state James Monroe succeeded Madison. The nation's fifth president, Monroe would preside over the Era of Good Feelings, a short but buoyant period of sectional harmony, growing prosperity, and strong nationalism. At this point, the fractious Federalists had virtually disappeared; business was good and getting better; handsome new buildings were rising in war-blackened Washington; money was safe with the new national bank; domestic trade was protected by a stern tariff; the frontier was moving west. In the resultant glow of national optimism, Monroe—who actually accomplished very little during his two terms—became one of America's most popular presidents.

For Calhoun, too, it seemed a golden time—particularly after the last election. The public had reacted with unexpected fury to a congressional pay increase—the legislators had more than doubled their old salaries, raising them to $1,500 per year—and most House members daring enough to run for reelection had been soundly defeated. Calhoun's advisers had told him to apologize to his constituents and to promise to roll back the raise if they reelected him.

Going his own way as usual, Calhoun refused the advice. He believed the new salaries barely enough to attract the best people to Congress; he was *not* sorry, and he would apologize to no one. Besides, he told his advisers, the people of South Carolina were intelligent. He would explain, they would understand, and he would return to Congress. He was right. The voters reelected him in a landslide.

Then he faced a new dilemma; Monroe offered him the post of secretary of war. When he received the job proposal, Calhoun was at Bath with his family—Floride, six-year-old Andrew, and Anna Maria, born the preceding February— and he spent three weeks struggling to reach a decision. The War Department, still in disarray after the 1812 conflict, was widely regarded as a no-win position for aspiring politicians. Calhoun's friends urged him to turn down the job, which would surely waste his "brilliant powers," but he saw things differently.

Calhoun wanted one day to become president. In Congress, he had earned a reputation as a brilliant debater, but he had no record as an administrator; running the War Department would change that. Reorganizing the department would both enhance his appeal as a presidential candidate and give him the opportunity to prepare the country for another war. He asked his wife to prepare for a move to the capital.

Calhoun took over the War Department in December 1817. He found the operation, he wrote later, "almost literally without organization, and everything in a state of confusion." The department had huge debts left over from the last war, no established military or Indian policies, no coherent regulations or procedures, no accounting system, no safeguards against graft. On paper, the army had 12,000 men; in reality, the figure was closer to 8,000.

Calhoun knew little about military science, but he was a fast learner. His first memo began, "We have much indeed to do." He spent a month reading every folder, file, and report in the office, then waded into his real task. Before the year was out, he had increased his headquarters staff, brought the army up to authorized strength, centralized the department's far-flung branches, and made sharp inroads on waste and fraud.

Calhoun's decisive performance as war secretary deeply impressed the president and other officials and military men; it also caught the public eye. As one newspaper observed: "The order and harmony, regularity and promptitude, punctuality and responsibility, introduced by Mr. Calhoun in every branch of the service has never been rivaled, and perhaps, cannot be excelled." Such remarks, of course, added luster to Calhoun's national reputation.

Always concerned about national defense, Calhoun proposed a massive program of coastal fort construction. To weaken British control over the western Indians, he suggested the deployment of American troops along the country's western frontier. He dispatched exploring expeditions to extend American influence into the Northwest. And, of course, he continued to press for his cherished network of roads and canals.

Calhoun made a point of exerting his authority over the often strong-willed officers under his command, but he ran into trouble with the Hero of New Orleans: Andrew Jackson was not called Old Hickory for nothing. Jackson "was invariably a problem," Calhoun biographer Coit has observed, "whether viewed close-up, over the sights of a dueling pistol, or at a distance Indian-hunting in Spanish territory." In the spring of 1818, Jackson was engaged in the latter occupation.

The general, then commander of the U.S. Army's Southern Division, invaded Spanish Florida in response to a series of murderous Seminole Indian raids into U.S. territory. Calhoun knew such an action could lead to war with the Spanish, the British, or both, and as secretary of war, he knew the United States was in no shape to fight. He ordered Jackson to "terminate the conflict," but the general misunderstood—or pretended to misunderstand—his orders from Washington. Roaring into Florida, he slaughtered countless Seminoles, took three Spanish forts, hanged two British traders, and captured the territory's Spanish governor.

News of Jackson's devastating Florida campaign divided the nation's capital into two camps. In one was Calhoun; extremely offended that Jackson had ignored his orders, the secretary of war demanded an investigation. Monroe agreed with Calhoun, but Secretary of State John Quincy Adams, an iron-willed, highly experienced diplomat (and son of the nation's second president), most emphatically did not.

The administration, insisted Adams, could not risk criticizing Jackson, a national hero and probably the most popular man in America. Furthermore, he said, the raid was just the sort of thing that would gain European respect for the United States. Finally, the secretary of state maintained, Jackson's raid would help persuade Spain to sell Florida to the United States.

After heated wrangling, the administration reached a unanimous decision: the forts would be returned to Spain, but the Hero of New Orleans would suffer no reprimand. The compromise had cost Calhoun the most, but he accepted it with grace. In a letter to Jackson written a few months later, he said, "I concur with you in regard . . . of the importance of Florida to the . . . security of our Southern frontier."

As a ranking member of the administration, Calhoun had a prominent social role in the capital. During the "Season" (when Congress was in session), dinners and dances at the Calhouns' large, rented house near the Capitol drew the cream of Washington society, the men dressed in somber splendor, the women gorgeously attired in white velvet, lace, and satin, wearing jeweled turbans or feathers in their hair. Both the Calhouns enjoyed wide personal popularity. Of John, one local society woman wrote, "Mr. Calhoun is a profound statesman and elegant scholar, but his manners . . . in private are endearing as well as captivating." Floride was described as a woman with "charming qualities: a devoted mother, tender wife, industrious, cheerful, intelligent, with the most perfectly equable temperament."

An old-world southerner, John Calhoun displayed impeccable manners: he was deferential to his seniors, easy but courteous with his peers, and sweepingly gallant to women of all ages. Friends sometimes tried to analyze just what made him such an attractive figure to so many people, but few had any luck defining him. He attracted others, one friend concluded lamely, "with a mystical something which is felt, but cannot be described."

Despite his social success, Calhoun preferred the company of his family and intimate friends to gala parties, and he truly enjoyed being with his children. "Anna Maria is a great talker," he noted in a letter to a friend in 1821, "and a source of much amusement to me." In another letter, he said, "Midst all of the anxiety which must occasionally be felt,

An 1819 British cartoon shows a pirate (Andrew Jackson) accepting "the government of the Floridas" from a grinning James Monroe. "There's your reward!" says the president. "Where e'er you catch the English string 'em up like herrings! Go, rob the Indians! Sell 'em for slaves!" Jackson's actions in Florida horrified Calhoun, but no one dared rebuke the Hero of New Orleans.

how much more happy you are with [your children], and how disconsolate you would be without them."

The Calhouns had arrived in Washington with two children, Andrew and Anna Maria. During her husband's seven years as war secretary, Floride gave birth to four more: Elizabeth, born in 1819; Patrick, 1821; John B., 1823; and Cornelia, 1824. Elizabeth, like her sister Floride, died of a sudden fever at the age of four months. Seven Calhoun children would reach adulthood, including James Edward and William Lowndes, who would arrive in 1826 and 1829, respectively.

Government officials (from the left) John Calhoun, Daniel Webster, Andrew Jackson, Henry Clay, and John Quincy Adams attend a Washington ball with their wives. In the political arena, Calhoun was known as a stern, even humorless, man, but offstage, he was admired for his wit, gallantry, and old-fashioned southern charm.

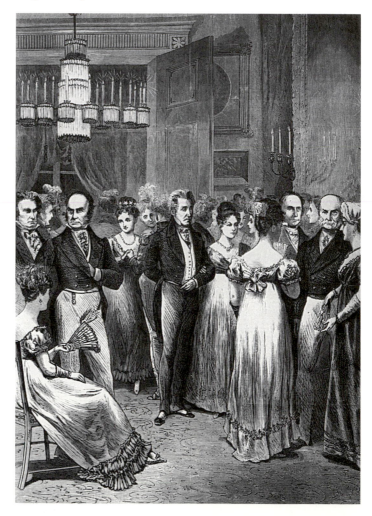

His children may have seen Calhoun as a gentle and amusing father, but others saw him as a driven man, even as a figure of destiny. As South Carolinian poet William J. Grayson put it, "There was a glare, a fire, in his eye, the fire of a soul that seemed to burn within him. It fascinated the beholder and rivetted his gaze." When Calhoun was not entertaining, he led an almost puritanical life, often spending 15 hours a day in his office. He also traveled widely, journeying by horseback or carriage to inspect fortifications, shipyards, military schools, and army bases from Boston to Charleston. He never worked as hard in his life as during his years as war secretary.

As Monroe began his second term of office in 1821, Calhoun weighed his chances of succeeding the president. He faced stiff competition: Secretary of State Adams, Congressman Henry Clay, and Secretary of the Treasury William H. Crawford had already thrown their hats into the ring. But Calhoun believed he could win. He felt certain that his rapid rise to prominence since 1811 and his performance as war secretary—brilliant, even in his opponents' judgment—had ensured him the support of the people.

Calhoun officially announced his presidential candidacy in December 1821. Despite the obvious disintegration of the Democratic Republican party into regional factions (Crawford represented the deep South, Clay the West, and Adams the Northeast), Calhoun presented himself as a national candidate. Thirty-nine years old and unshakably confident in himself and his ability to sway the voters, he declared, "I belong to no section or particular interest. It has been my pride to be . . . devoted to the great interests of the country."

*Easily elected vice-president in 1824, the 42-year-old Calhoun imme-
diately began opposing President John Quincy Adams. He planned
to help Andrew Jackson replace Adams after one term, serve as Jackson's vice-president for four years, then gain the presidency himself.*

6

Nullification

IN THE FALL OF 1823, 56-year-old Andrew Jackson gave in to his admirers and agreed to run for president. Across the country, Democratic Republicans responded with cheers; what America needed, they said, was "a single illustrious individual"—Old Hickory, the mighty Hero of New Orleans. Jackson looked unbeatable; his move stopped Calhoun's presidential aspirations in their tracks.

The end, for the moment at least, of Calhoun's hopes for the White House left him disappointed but not discouraged. Although he claimed to care "nothing" about the vice-presidency, he knew the post could serve as a stepping-stone to the White House. At this point in American history, presidential elections did not operate as they do today. The first difference, of course, was one of gender and race: all candidates, all office holders, and all voters were free, white, and male. (Black males would technically gain the right to vote with the passage of the Fifteenth Amendment to the Constitution in 1870; women were not to receive the

Andrew Jackson presents a dashing image after his stunning 1815 victory over the British in New Orleans. Although the wildly popular general won the greatest number of votes in the presidential election of 1824, he failed to receive a clear majority, throwing the final decision into the House of Representatives. There he lost to Adams, thanks to a deal—the so-called corrupt bargain—struck by Adams and Speaker of the House Henry Clay.

right to vote until 1920.) Contenders for the highest office could be, and often were, members of the same party. Each could endorse a vice-presidential candidate, but his choice did not bind the voters; if a citizen chose to do so, he could vote for a chief executive from one party and a second-in-command from another.

In the campaign of 1824—one of the bitterest ever held in the United States—four men ran for president: Secretary of State John Quincy Adams, who defined himself as an "independent Federalist," and three so-called Democratic Republicans: Senator Andrew Jackson (the Tennessee state legislature had appointed him to fill a U.S. Senate vacancy in 1823), Speaker of the House Henry Clay, and Treasury Secretary William H. Crawford. As a running mate, both Adams and Jackson had endorsed John C. Calhoun, nominally a Democratic Republican.

The South Carolinian quickly became the clear favorite in his contest, but the presidential race looked murkier. When the votes were counted in the fall of 1824, Jackson was seen to have won the most: 153,500. Adams came in next, with 108,700, followed by Clay with 47,100 and Crawford with 46,600. According to U.S. law, then and now, popular votes translated into electoral votes, ballots cast in the electoral college by delegates pledged to vote for particular candidates. If an absolute majority of votes was not received by any candidate in the electoral college, the final decision was to be made by the House of Representatives.

Jackson received 99 electoral votes to Adams's 84, Crawford's 41, and Clay's 37; as none represented a clear majority, the House was obliged to decide between the three candidates with the highest number of votes. Crawford dropped out for health reasons, and Clay was not among the top three, leaving Jackson and Adams.

As Speaker of the House, Clay wielded enormous influence, and Clay had no love for the popular hero. "I cannot believe," he said, "that killing 2,500 Englishmen at New Orleans qualifies a person" for the presidency. After a private conversation with Adams, Clay swung his support to the New Englander; on February 9, 1825, Adams became the nation's sixth president by the slender majority of 13 of the 25 states.

When Adams shortly afterward named Clay as his secretary of state, outraged Jacksonians shouted, "Corrupt bargain!" Calhoun agreed. Six days after Adams's inauguration, the new vice-president wrote to a close friend about Clay's appointment: "The voice and the power of the people has been set at naught," he asserted, "and the result has been a President elected not by them, but a few ambitious men with a view to their own interest."

Adams's first message to Congress outlined a program bearing the unmistakable stamp of Clay's American System. Calhoun, although he still agreed with most parts of the program, had become disenchanted with protective tariffs. Just before the election, Congress had passed a tariff with rates almost twice as high as those Calhoun had supported in 1816. At about the same time, cotton prices had fallen sharply on the international market, throwing the southeastern states into an economic depression worse than that of 1819.

Southern planters blamed their problems on the tariff, which protected northern industries from foreign competition and drove the prices of manufactured goods up, while southern cotton earned planters less and less money with which to pay for them. Calhoun, for his part, regarded the Tariff of 1824 as a blatant move by the manufacturing interests of the north to enrich themselves at the expense of the agricultural states of his home region.

Calhoun's political ambitions helped to drive him further into opposition to his own administration. He suspected Clay of trying to succeed Adams as president by exploiting the American System's popularity in western and northern states. Calhoun decided to block Clay by throwing his considerable influence in the South behind Jackson, even if that meant handing Jackson the election of 1828. Neither

Calhoun nor any other astute observer doubted that Jackson would easily defeat Adams in the next campaign. Calhoun also believed that Jackson, if elected, would serve only one term (at the end of a term starting in 1829, Jackson would be 66 years old), and he felt confident that if he supported him now, he could sail into the presidency in 1832 as Old Hickory's heir apparent.

After taking over as Adams's vice-president (which also made him president of the Senate), Calhoun set about organizing the anti-administration forces in Congress. He took advantage of his position in the Senate to place Jackson supporters in positions of power. He also enforced Senate debating rules loosely, allowing his old enemy Jack Randolph, now a senator, to attack Adams and Clay with extraordinary venom; so bitter were the remarks of Mad Jack, in fact, that Clay challenged the old Virginian to a duel.

Calhoun found himself unable to prevent Clay and Randolph from meeting at a secluded spot along the Potomac to exchange pistol shots. Fortunately, no one was hurt in the April 1826 duel. Unfortunately, Randolph continued to hurl insults across the Senate floor at Clay and anyone else who displeased him. Sometimes, one of those who displeased him was John Calhoun. At one point, Randolph began a speech by shouting, "Mr. Speaker! I mean Mr. President of the Senate and would-be President of the United States, which God in his infinite mercy prevent."

Calhoun found an unlikely political ally in Treasury Secretary Crawford's former campaign manager, Senator Martin Van Buren of New York. Although northern and protariff, the diminutive, well-dressed Van Buren shared the South Carolinian's desire to hamstring Clay. Van Buren enlisted Calhoun's aid in building a coalition of northerners and southerners to support Jackson. Although Calhoun suspected Van Buren of plotting to succeed Jackson himself, he cooperated with the New Yorker in welding some of the fragments of the old Democratic Republican party into an opposition political organization.

On June 4, 1826, Calhoun wrote to Jackson and formally offered to help him defeat Adams in 1828. Jackson accepted and told Calhoun to consider himself his running mate. Calhoun's change in political alignment left him feeling somewhat uncomfortable. In a letter to former president Monroe he wrote, "Never in any country, in my opinion, was there in so short a period, so complete an anarchy of political relations. Every prominent public man feels that he has been thrown into a new attitude, and has to re-examine his new position, and reapply principles to the situation into which he was so unexpectedly and suddenly thrown."

Cotton prices continued to fall, and southern anger over the tariff grew, particularly in South Carolina. Many southerners threatened secession if Washington refused to lower tariff rates. Calhoun worried about the effect of the controversy on his presidential ambitions. If the South came out in favor of disunion, reaction in the North could ruin the Jackson-Calhoun ticket's chances in 1828 and dash his hopes of succeeding Jackson as president. Despite his fears, however, Calhoun did not hesitate to use his power as president of the Senate to show where his sympathies lay. When a Senate vote on a bill to raise the tariff on imported woolen products ended in a tie in February 1827, Calhoun unhesitatingly cast the tie-breaking vote to kill the bill.

During the winter of 1827, administration supporters in Congress introduced a bill to raise tariff rates. Van Buren then devised a plan to destroy the measure: he would attach to the tariff bill a rider (a second proposal, which can "ride" to victory on the coattails of the original). Van Buren's rider, he explained to Calhoun, would raise import fees on several materials—iron, hemp, and molasses, for example—necessary to New England rum distillers and shipbuilders. Alarmed by the prospect of the high new duties, representatives of the New England states would vote against the rider, which would automatically defeat the tariff bill on which it was "riding."

The ploy met with Calhoun's approval, but then, to his dismay, Van Buren defected, casting his vote for an

Martin Van Buren, the same age as Calhoun and equally ambitious, was different in every other respect. Tall and outspoken, Calhoun made no secret of his opinions or objectives—and had no shortage of enemies as a result—but he failed to achieve some of his most cherished goals. The short, red-haired Van Buren (also known as the Little Magician and the Red Fox) spoke softly, gave offense to no one, and smoothly accomplished most of his aims.

administration amendment that would make the bill more palatable to the New Englanders. The tariff bill squeaked through the Senate, and President Adams signed it into law in May 1828.

The passage of the Tariff of 1828—the "Tariff of Abominations," as it came to be known in the South—ignited a fire storm of controversy. Calhoun charged Van Buren with treachery. The bill, he raged, represented nothing less than a concerted effort by the North to destroy the South's slave-based agricultural plantation society and turn it into a manufacturing society along northern lines.

While spending the summer at Fort Hill, his new residence overlooking the Seneca River in southwestern South Carolina (on what are now the grounds of Clemson University), Calhoun received a request from the South Carolina legislature for a report on the Tariff of 1828. He lost no time in complying. He had already thought at length about the problem posed by the tariff, namely that of protecting a minority—in this case, the South—from domination by a majority—in this case, the northerners who controlled the federal government. He saw the report as a chance to outline a constitutional solution to the problem that would protect southern society while defusing calls for the South to secede from the Union.

In November 1828, Calhoun produced a document that the state legislature later published as the *South Carolina Exposition and Protest*. He kept his authorship secret in order to avoid damaging his image in northern states. The *Exposition* began by declaring the Tariff of 1828 unconstitutional; in Calhoun's opinion the federal government had the right to impose duties only in order to raise operating revenue and support the general welfare, not to protect the interests of a particular region.

Calhoun went on to outline the dangers inherent in what he called the "tyranny" of majority rule. "Irresponsible power," he asserted, "is inconsistent with liberty, and must corrupt those who exercise it." Foreshadowing the work of

German social theorist Karl Marx (1818–83), he predicted the division of the country into capitalists and workers if the abuses of federal power by the northern manufacturing interests were not reversed, and foresaw a time when the workers would be barely able to afford the necessities of life.

Drawing on the writings of James Madison and Thomas Jefferson, Calhoun proposed a system for protecting minority rights under the Constitution. He declared that a state had the right to nullify (declare invalid) a federal law that it considered unconstitutional; that state, said Calhoun, had merely to call a popularly elected state convention to declare the law void. To enact a law over such a state action, Congress and three-fourths of the states would have to amend the Constitution to specifically grant the federal government the power in question.

"All controversy between the States and the general Government would thus be adjusted," Calhoun maintained, "and the Constitution would gradually acquire by its constant interposition in important cases, all the perfection of which the work of man is susceptible." Calhoun ended with a warning that if the next president did not lower the tariff, South Carolina would have "a duty to herself—to the Union—to the present, and to future generations—and to the cause of liberty over the world" to nullify it.

The Jackson-Calhoun ticket, representing the new Democratic party, easily defeated Adams and his National Republicans in the November 1828 elections. Calhoun, however, found his position with the new president less secure than he had thought. Jackson appointed Van Buren secretary of state and a Van Buren supporter, Tennessee senator John H. Eaton, secretary of war. Calhoun managed to have his choice for the State Department, Littleton Tazewell of Virginia, named ambassador to Great Britain, and gained the Treasury Department for another supporter, Samuel Ingham.

When Jackson failed to offer any tariff concessions to the South in his first message to Congress, Calhoun grew more

A list of Ohio electors pledged to the Jackson-Calhoun slate appears under the party's 1828 motto: "To sweep the Augean stable," meaning to clean up an enormous mess. Voters went for the ticket in record numbers, whisking Adams and his National-Republicans from the White House and replacing them with Jackson, Calhoun, and the Democratic-Republicans.

To sweep the Augean Stable.

FOR PRESIDENT,
Andrew Jackson.

FOR VICE-PRESIDENT,
JOHN C. CALHOUN.

ETHAN ALLEN BROWN, of Hamilton
ROBERT HARPER, Ashtabula.
WILLIAM PIATT, Hamilton.
JAMES SHIELDS, Butler.
HENRY BARRINGTON, Miami.
THOMAS GILLESPIE, Green.
THOMAS L. HAMER, Brown,
VALENTINE KEFFER, Pickaway.
ROBERT LUCAS, Pike.
JOHN M'ELVAIN, Franklin.
SAMUEL HERRICK, Muskingum.
GEORGE SHARP, Belmont.
WALTER M. BLAKE, Tuscarawas.
BENJAMIN JONES, Wayne.
WILLIAM RAYEN, Trumbull.
HUGH M' FALL, Richland.

Lampooning the turbulent Jackson administration, an 1831 political cartoon shows Jackson seated on a collapsing chair. Van Buren is the rat at lower left, threatened by an American eagle who guards a ladder representing the nation. "If I could only humbug that eagle and climb up this ladder," says Van Buren. "You don't get up if I can help it," growls Calhoun, the terrier next to him. Meanwhile, Webster (at the window, left), observes, "That terrier has nullified the whole Concern."

suspicious of Van Buren. His efforts to block the New Yorker's influence over the president were complicated, however, by a social scandal that rapidly enveloped the new administration; it concerned Secretary of War Eaton's new wife, the former Peggy O'Neal Timberlake. The beautiful 29-year-old daughter of a tavernkeeper, Peggy Eaton was widely regarded in Washington society as a woman of loose morals. Ignoring Jackson's heated defense of Mrs. Eaton's virtue and his orders that she be accepted, Calhoun's wife led a movement among the prominent women of the capital to ostracize her. Calhoun feared repercussions in his relationship with the president, but bowed to Floride's social authority. Van Buren, however, solidified his relationship with the president at Calhoun's expense by openly socializing with the Eatons.

To further discredit Calhoun, Van Buren dug up the South Carolinian's attempt, while secretary of war, to censure Jackson. A letter from President Monroe to Calhoun on the subject had fallen into Jackson's hands before the election of 1828, but the old general had tabled it to avoid disrupting the campaign. After the election, Van Buren obtained a statement from a former colleague in the Monroe cabinet, confirming that Calhoun had attempted to punish Jackson. When the president confronted Calhoun with the statement, Calhoun was forced to admit that he had kept the truth about the incident hidden.

Jackson also suspected Calhoun of being behind the nullification doctrine. Word had leaked out of his authorship of the *South Carolina Exposition and Protest*. To make matters worse, Senator Robert Y. Hayne of South Carolina had argued in favor of nullification during a great debate in the Senate with Daniel Webster in January 1830, with Calhoun nodding his support from the president's chair.

The break between Calhoun and Jackson became public at a dinner in honor of Jefferson's birthday held at Brown's Indian Queen Hotel in Washington on April 13, 1830. Jackson, giving the first toast, glared at Calhoun and declared, "Our Federal Union: It must be preserved." Calhoun, next in line, replied, "The Union: Next to our liberty, most dear. May we all remember that it can only be preserved by respecting the rights of the states and by distributing equally the benefits and burdens of the Union."

Despite Jackson's declared intent to seek a second term, Calhoun harbored hopes of winning the presidential election of 1832 on his own. As in 1824, he convinced himself that he remained popular in the country as a whole. Developments in his home state, however, permanently shattered his illusions. A radical nullification movement had grown up in South Carolina in response to the Tariff of 1828, led by Governor James Hamilton and a former protégé of Calhoun's, Congressman George McDuffie. The radicals quickly gained the support of a majority of the planters and farmers in the state. In May 1831, McDuffie gave a dramatic speech in Charleston demanding nullification of the hated tariff at all costs, even if it meant secession.

McDuffie's speech brought home to Calhoun that the forces he had unleashed with the *South Carolina Exposition and Protest* were threatening to explode. If he failed to gain control of the radical movement and guide it into peaceful, constitutional channels while keeping up the pressure on Jackson to lower the tariff, he would lose the leadership in South Carolina, which was vital to his political future. He wrote to Treasury Secretary Ingham, "I see clearly [that McDuffie's speech] brings matters to a crisis, and that I must meet it promptly and manfully."

To gain control of the situation in South Carolina, Calhoun had to identify himself openly as a nullifier—which was synonymous with "traitor" in many parts of the country—and give up all hopes of reaching the presidency quickly. On July 26, 1831, the Pendleton, South Carolina, *Messenger* published an address from Calhoun written at Fort Hill. It stated the case for nullification in clear, persuasive terms that transformed the impassioned declarations of the radicals into a reasoned political theory. Daniel Webster, on reading the Fort Hill Address, remarked that it "was the ablest and most plausible, and therefore the most dangerous vindication of that particular form of Revolution which has yet appeared."

In his message to Congress of December 1831, President Jackson promised to reduce the tariff to encourage the pro-Union party in South Carolina. The following summer, however, Henry Clay, who was running against Jackson at the head of the National Republican ticket, sponsored a tariff bill that, while lowering rates, remained protective. Jackson did not dare veto the bill in an election year for fear of losing his support in northern states. The Tariff of 1832 did not placate the South Carolina radicals. In November 1832, a state convention passed an ordinance nullifying the tariffs of 1828 and 1832 in South Carolina as of February 1, 1833.

An 1832 lithograph shows a Washington landmark, Brown's Indian Queen Hotel. In a banquet held here in 1830, Jackson had glowered at Calhoun and proposed a toast directly aimed at his vice-president's doctrine of nullification: "Our Federal Union: It must be preserved." Calhoun bowed politely and then offered a salute he knew would enrage the president. "The Union," he said, "Next to our liberty, most dear."

Jackson, his soldier's instincts aroused, called the nullification doctrine "treasonous," and threatened to use military force to collect the tariff duties.

The radicals responded by recalling Senator Hayne from Washington to serve as the state's governor, and by electing Calhoun to replace him and defend their actions in the Senate. As Jackson sent reinforcements to federal forts in Charleston harbor and tensions between pro- and anti-nullification forces in South Carolina mounted, Calhoun traveled to Columbia to confer with Hayne and former governor Hamilton. On December 28, 1832, he sent a letter of resignation to Jackson. He then set out for Washington to defend his state before the Senate and the country.

This likeness of the "cast-iron man," sketched as he addressed the Senate in the 1830s, appeared in the political magazine Democratic Review. *It was British writer Harriet Martineau who gave Calhoun the "cast-iron" label; he looked "as if he had never been born and could never be extinguished," she said, adding that she knew "of no one who lives in such utter intellectual solitude."*

7

The Cast-Iron Man

CALHOUN JOURNEYED TO WASHINGTON amid rumors that President Jackson planned to arrest him on charges of treason if South Carolina resisted the tariff by force. Shortly after Calhoun took his seat in the Senate on January 4, 1833, the president asked Congress for the authority to use the army and the navy against the nullifiers. On January 21, the Senate Judiciary Committee reported a bill giving Jackson the power he asked for. Southerners instantly dubbed the measure the Force Bill.

Calhoun bitterly denounced what he called the "bloody act" and promised to resist it "at every hazard—even that of death itself." On January 22, he introduced a series of resolutions in the Senate that echoed the *South Carolina Exposition and Protest*. In them, he declared that the people of the United States did not form a single nation; the Constitution instead represented a pact between sovereign states, which retained both the first loyalty of their citizens and the right to decide the constitutionality of federal laws.

In mid-February, Calhoun clashed with Daniel Webster in one of the Senate's epic debates. Weak and feverish from tension, Calhoun attacked the Force Bill before a packed Senate chamber in a speech that lasted two days. He coldly reviewed his arguments on the dangers of majority rule, calling Jackson a tyrant and asserting that the Force Bill threatened both the integrity of the states and the liberty of their citizens. The soaring rhetoric of Webster's reply contrasted sharply with Calhoun's unemotional logic. Webster argued for the supremacy of the federal government and declared, "The truth is . . . that, as to certain purposes, the people of the United States are one people."

In his response to Webster, Calhoun revealed for the first time the true roots of the nullification crisis. He warned that the power claimed for the federal government by the Force Bill would provide "a pretext to interfere with our political affairs and domestic institutions in a manner infinitely more dangerous than any other power which has ever been exercised," a clear reference to slavery. By widening the debate to include slavery, Calhoun made it clear that he and his followers regarded nullification as their only defense against a hostile northern majority bent on using federal power to destroy not only southern agriculture but the entire southern way of life.

Calhoun realized, however, that he had little hope of defeating the Force Bill. He began instead to work for a tariff reduction that would defuse the crisis short of civil war. He found an unlikely ally in Henry Clay, who shared his opposition to Jackson. Congress was already considering an administration measure designed to pacify South Carolina by slashing tariff rates. Calhoun and Clay, unwilling to let Jackson and Van Buren take credit for keeping the peace, countered with a compromise bill that reduced tariffs slowly over a 10-year period. The measure, drafted by Clay, lowered tariffs to the level of 1816 while shielding northern industries from the shock of a sudden loss of tariff protection.

With Calhoun's support, Clay's compromise easily passed both houses of Congress. When the Force Bill came up for a vote in the Senate, however, Calhoun and eight of his supporters walked out of the chamber. Despite their defiant gesture, the bill passed on March 1 with only a single dissenting vote. The next day, Jackson signed both the Force Bill and the compromise tariff into law.

Calhoun rushed backed to Columbia to persuade the nullification convention to accept the compromise. So

Concluding a Senate speech with the words, "Liberty and Union, now and forever, one and inseparable!" Daniel Webster leaves his colleagues spellbound.

great was his fear that it would refuse and trigger federal military action that he risked his already strained health by traveling in an open mail wagon along the icy roads. On March 11, he arrived in the state capital and found the convention in session. The radicals agreed to accept the compromise and voted to repeal the nullification ordinance. As a face-saving gesture, the convention passed an ordinance nullifying the Force Bill.

Calhoun proclaimed the compromise a triumphant success for nullification. In March 1833, he wrote to his former assistant at the War Department, Christopher Vandeventer: the tariff system "has got its death wound blow," he said. "Nullification has dealt the fatal blow . . . there shall be at least one free State." Despite his public exultation, however, Calhoun recognized that South Carolina would be unable to stand alone in the face of Jackson's threats. No other southern state had come forward to support nullification. Consequently, Calhoun began to work for southern unity, trying to persuade the southern states to join him in defending their way of life.

Throughout Jackson's second term of office, Calhoun continued to cooperate with the anti-administration forces in Congress. Jackson's attempts to assert the powers of his office both during and after the nullification crisis had created a strong opposition movement, which coalesced under Clay's leadership into a group calling itself the Whig party. Calhoun did not formally join the Whigs, preferring instead to remain at the head of a small proslavery, states' rights party.

The growth of the abolitionist, or antislavery, movement in the northern states during the 1830s provided Calhoun with plenty of ammunition for his appeal to southern unity. Although they represented only a small minority of the population, the abolitionists had become highly visible. Antislavery societies sent petitions to Congress demanding the abolition of the interstate slave trade and of slavery in the territories and in the District of Columbia. They also

Terse and powerful, "Am I not a man and a brother?" proved one of the New England abolitionists' most effective weapons. The bold woodcut image of a chained slave, originated by the British antislavery movement in the 1780s, appeared on thousands of American posters and handbills from the 1830s on.

began to mail southerners a flood of pamphlets that aimed at inciting slave uprisings.

At a meeting called in Pendleton, South Carolina, in September 1835 to discuss the problem of abolitionist mailings, Calhoun helped write a report that declared, "The liberty of the press implies no privilege to disturb by seditious libels, the peace of the community—to throw firebrands amidst a peaceful and unoffending people." He responded to a petition presented by Senator John Tipton of Indiana in February 1837 demanding the abolition of slavery in the District of Columbia by asking the Senate not to receive any more such petitions. He eventually managed to persuade his colleagues to adopt a "gag rule" that automatically tabled them without debate.

Calhoun had justified his position before the Senate with broad arguments in defense of slavery:

> There has never yet existed a wealthy and civilized
> society in which one portion of the community did not,
> in the point of fact, live on the labor of the other . . .
> I fearlessly assert that the existing relation between the
> two races in the South, against which these blind fanatics
> [the abolitionists] are waging war, forms the most solid
> foundation on which to rear free and stable political
> institutions.

Calhoun appealed to southerners to unite in the face of the northern threat: "If we do not defend ourselves none will defend; if we yield we will be more and more pressed as we recede; and if we submit we will be trampled underfoot," he declared. United, he added, the South could "find ample means of security without resorting to secession or disunion."

Calhoun failed, however, to unite the southern states behind him. Instead, he played into the hands of the abolitionists by making their cause more visible, and angered moderate northerners by attacking the constitutional guarantees of free speech and petition. His failure was symbolized by Van Buren's victory in the presidential election of 1836, which left Calhoun where he had started, as the leader of a small, radical faction in the Senate.

Calhoun made a strong impression on those who met him during this period. In an account published in 1839, a young German who visited the controversial Carolinian in Washington wrote:

> As he was explaining his views and theories, which . . .
> he did in the most concise manner, and with a degree
> of rapidity which required our utmost attention to follow
> him, his face assumed an almost supernatural expression;
> his dark brows were knit together, his eyes shot fire, his
> black hair stood on end, while on his quivering lips there
> hung an almost Mephistophelean scorn at the absurdity of
> the opposite doctrine. Then, at once, he became again all
> calmness, gentleness, and good nature, laughing at the
> blunders of his friends and foes.

An Englishwoman, the traveler and social critic Harriet Martineau, described him in 1838 as

> the cast-iron man, who looks as if he had never been
> born and could never be extinguished. . . . He meets men,
> and harangues them by the fireside as in the Senate . . .
> he either passes by what you say, or twists it into a
> suitability with what is in his head, and begins to lecture
> again. . . . Relaxation is no longer in the power of his will.
> I never saw anyone who so completely gave me the idea
> of possession.

Calhoun began to have some doubts in the wake of the elections of 1836 about his marriage of convenience to the Whigs. Clay continued to support broad federal powers that might be used to restrict or even abolish slavery, and Calhoun suspected him of catering to the northern anti-slavery vote. With Jackson out of office, Calhoun decided that he could better achieve his goals by returning to the Democrats. In September 1837, he openly supported Presi-

dent Van Buren on a bill to replace the Bank of the United States with an independent treasury system. Two years later, he formally rejoined the Democratic party.

Calhoun's change of political course, which John Quincy Adams called his "bargain and sale of himself to Van Buren," exposed him to a storm of criticism and threatened to alienate him from his supporters. He defended himself by claiming that he had only aided the Whigs to oppose Jackson's rule, and that the Democrats more truly reflected his opinions. In a dramatic debate in early 1838, both Clay and Webster charged Calhoun with having trimmed his sails for personal political gain. Calhoun ably returned their fire, sarcastically pointing out their vulnerability to the same charges. The controversy nonetheless hurt public confidence in Calhoun's consistency and political motives.

The aftermath of the presidential campaign of 1840, however, gave Calhoun renewed hope for the future. The

In 1835, the citizens of Charleston, South Carolina, raided the post office and burned such antislavery mailings as the Liberator *found there. Abolitionists mailed southerners material intended to incite slave revolts and sent petitions to Congress demanding the end of the interstate slave trade. Calhoun persuaded his colleagues to automatically table such petitions.*

Whig victor, General William Henry Harrison of Ohio, died after a month in office, and his successor, Vice-President John Tyler of Virginia, broke with the Whig leadership over a bill to recharter the Bank of the United States. An outraged Clay and his followers read Tyler out of the Whig party, forcing the president to turn to Calhoun for support.

Calhoun saw himself leading the Democratic party to victory in 1844 against the rapidly disintegrating Whigs. He wrote to a member of the South Carolina legislature in November 1841, "If my friends should think my services ever will be of importance at the head of the Executive, now is the time." In the closing days of 1842, South Carolina unanimously nominated Calhoun for the presidency, followed shortly thereafter by Georgia. In March 1843, Calhoun retired from the Senate to devote his energies to his campaign.

One month before Calhoun's retirement, Harper and Brothers of New York published a short biography of him, together with a collection of his speeches. The biography presented Calhoun as a leader of the highest ideals and referred to him as "the master-statesman of his age." Although he was not named as the author, Calhoun had in fact written most of the book himself and had approved the rest. The ploy had little effect. His campaign fell victim to his inflexible stand on slavery and his reputation for political opportunism. In 1843, he lost the Virginia and New York Democratic nominations to Van Buren. By 1844, he was out of the race.

It was the controversy over the admission of Texas to the Union that determined the outcome of the presidential race of 1844. The Lone Star Republic had gained independence from Mexico in 1836, and public opinion in both the United States and Texas strongly favored annexation. When Van Buren failed to commit himself on the issue, he lost the Democratic nomination to James K. Polk, the former governor of Tennessee and a Jackson supporter. Polk's strong stand in favor of annexation helped him to carry the election over his Whig opponent, Clay.

Calhoun supported the admission of Texas, which permitted slavery, to the Union. As he saw it, the vast southwestern republic would provide the southern states with the parity in territory and population they needed to defend their institutions in Congress. In early 1844, President Tyler asked Calhoun to join his cabinet as secretary of state. Calhoun, perceiving an opportunity to help the annexation process, accepted.

On taking over the State Department, Calhoun found a note from the British foreign secretary, Lord Aberdeen. His nation, declared Aberdeen, not only opposed slavery (the British Empire had abolished it in 1833) but intended to help end the practice in all the world's countries, including the Republic of Texas. Calhoun, who suspected the British government of plotting to destroy the plantation system of the South for the benefit of its own agricultural colonies, wrote a stiff letter in reply.

In this 1844 cartoon, former president Andrew Jackson cuts the branch that supports Whig candidate Henry Clay (nicknamed "that old coon") and his running mate. Below them is Democratic candidate James K. Polk, who prompts Clay to wail, "My struggles are of no avail / For Polk has got me by the tail." Meanwhile, Calhoun (left) and three other "Democratic dogs" bark, "Down with the coons." Clay lost the 1844 election to Polk.

The United States, said Calhoun, would annex Texas in order to protect slavery. He then went on to defend slavery as beneficial both to slaves and to their masters. He supported his claims with statistics purporting to show that feeblemindedness and insanity were more common among the free blacks of the North than among the slaves of the South.

Although the letter contained little that Calhoun had not already said in the Senate, he did not intend for it to reach the public. Nonetheless, the New York *Evening Post*, a pro–Van Buren newspaper, obtained a copy and promptly printed it. The letter convinced many northerners that proslavery forces were behind the annexation movement. As a result of the controversy, the Senate voted down an annexation treaty that Calhoun had negotiated with the Texas government.

The annexationists in Congress nonetheless managed to bring Texas into the Union by a joint resolution of both houses. It was signed into law by President Polk on March 1, 1845. The maneuver required a very broad, even dubious interpretation of the Constitution, which gives the Senate the exclusive right to approve treaties. Despite his normally strict views on the Constitution, Calhoun gave his support to the tactic in order to circumvent the two-thirds vote requirement. (A joint resolution only needs a simple majority of both houses for passage.)

At the height of the battle over Texas, Calhoun fell seriously ill with pulmonary pneumonia. He recovered under the care of his wife, his youngest daughter Cornelia (whom a childhood accident had left crippled and barely able to walk), and his niece Eugenia, but the disease left him seriously weakened. On February 18, the Philadelphia lawyer Francis Wharton visited Calhoun and was shocked by what he saw. "As he rose to meet me," Wharton later recalled, "I was much struck with the emaciation of his frame, and the feebleness of his gait. . . . His eye was glazed, his cheek hectic, and his voice broken by cough."

Despite his poor health, Calhoun hoped that he would be asked to continue as secretary of state in the Polk administration. The new president instead offered him the post of ambassador to Great Britain, a move designed to get the controversial southern statesman out of the country, gain the support of Van Buren, and reconcile the factions within the Democratic party. Calhoun refused the bait. He wrote bitterly to his daughter that he would instead retire to Fort Hill, "with the good will of all, including the administration, and the regret, I may say, of almost the whole country, with no small censure on the administration, for not inviting me to continue."

By 1845, Calhoun's hair had become white and his face gaunt, but the man himself—described by a friend as "too intellectual, too industrious, too intent in the struggle of politics"—remained unchanged. At the age of 63, the tireless South Carolinian began preparing another campaign for the goal that had so long eluded him, the presidency of the United States.

8

A Nation Divided

CALHOUN STILL CHERISHED hopes for the presidency. The recognition he received on his journey back to South Carolina convinced him that his hour would strike in the elections of 1848. At a dinner held in his honor in Richmond, Virginia, the state's Democratic politicians toasted him as their next presidential candidate. He received similar expressions of support in Charleston. When Calhoun reached home on March 21, 1845, he began laying the groundwork for his campaign.

Calhoun divided his time at Fort Hill between politics and farming. The plantation, which he had originally rented from his mother-in-law, had become his property when she died in April 1836. Of Fort Hill's 1,000 acres of rolling countryside, 450 were under cultivation, producing corn and cotton as well as oats, wheat, potatoes, and rice. What land remained Calhoun turned over to orchards, pastures, and forest. To work his fields Calhoun kept between 70 and 80 slaves, including his boyhood companion, now known as Old Sawney.

Calhoun was by all accounts a humane master and a superb plantation manager. He applied the same self-confidence, analytical skills, and passion for logic to farming that he had brought to Senate debates. He experimented with new crops and new farming techniques in an effort to help other farmers in the region to boost their productivity, and he constantly sought to improve his own management.

Calhoun did not gain as much pleasure from his family as he did from farming. In the aftermath of a stroke, suffered in the summer of 1842, Floride Calhoun had changed radically, both in appearance and disposition. Now seriously overweight, she had also become (as her husband confided in a letter to a friend) "suspicious and fault-finding." Writing to his daughter Anna Maria, Calhoun called her mother's volatile personality "the only cross of my life." He treated Floride with as much patience and kindness as he could muster, but the marriage had lost its joy.

Adding to Calhoun's burdens were his seven surviving children, not all of whom rose to the heights he had once envisioned for them. By 1848, 37-year-old Andrew had been expelled from Yale for misconduct and had tried—and

At his beloved Fort Hill home (seen in a photograph taken about 1880), Calhoun exercised his farming skills and enjoyed life. With its rolling hills and lazy river, its orchards and giant oaks, its rich pastures and fields, the plantation brought the old political warrior a sense of peace he found nowhere else on earth.

Cotton planter Andrew Pickens Calhoun, notes biographer Margaret Coit, "unfortunately inherited all of his father's indifference to money, with little of his scrupulousness in the use of it." The first of John and Floride's children, Andrew remained his father's favorite despite his sometimes difficult behavior.

failed at—a number of occupations. When he decided to found a plantation in Alabama, his father borrowed large sums of money to help him get started, but the project soon failed, victim of depressed cotton prices and Andrew's own ineptitude as a manager. The debacle left Calhoun deeply in debt.

West Point graduate Patrick, the Calhouns' second son, enjoyed only moderate success as an army officer, partly because of his fondness for drinking and gambling. To protect the family's name, the elder Calhoun frequently found himself covering Patrick's large debts. By 1848, John C. Calhoun, Jr., who had attended various colleges, finally earned a medical degree. At this point, the youngest Calhouns, James Edward and William Lowndes, settled down to attend the South Carolina College in Columbia.

Calhoun's eldest daughter, Anna Maria, came the closest to fulfilling his expectations. Dark haired, dark eyed, and

A champion to the South, Calhoun was a monster to the North; here, he rips helpless "free staters" from their beds and bites their heads off. But negative feelings about the intense, unshakeable South Carolinian were not limited to the North. In 1837, a decade after he chose Calhoun as his running mate, Andrew Jackson said he had one regret in life: "that I have not . . . hanged John C. Calhoun."

musically talented as her mother had been, she alone of all the children seemed to have inherited her father's intelligence; she often discussed politics with him and became his closest confidante.

Calhoun's 1844 battle with pneumonia left him with the appearance he would retain for the rest of his life. A thick mane of iron-gray hair framed his emaciated face, with its square chin, bushy eyebrows, and piercing eyes. He continued to impress others as a humorless, high-strung thinking machine. Senator Dixon H. Lewis of Alabama, who idolized him, wrote, "Calhoun . . . is too intellectual, too industrious, too intent in the struggle of politics to suit me except as an occasional companion. There is no relaxation in him." Others, however, saw a more charismatic side to his personality. A freshman congressman who met Calhoun for the first time in 1844 wrote, "He was the most charming man in conversation I ever heard."

Most people, including his supporters, agreed that although Calhoun had undeniable gifts as a statesman, he had little talent for politics. His inconsistency had more than once cost him what had seemed certain political success. One of his friends, Judge Beverly Tucker of Virginia, once ruefully declared, "How [Calhoun] might manage the affairs of a great nation I do not know, but he certainly is the most unskillful leader of a party that ever wielded a truncheon."

Calhoun's actions between 1845 and the elections of 1848 proved Tucker's point. In the fall of 1845, at a convention in Memphis, Tennessee, the South Carolina politician shocked his supporters by calling for the federal government to help build a network of railroads, turnpikes, and canals between the southern and western states. Calhoun saw the scheme as a way to realize his dream of uniting the South and West in a bond of common interest, but those who had followed him under the banner of states' rights and a weak federal government saw this apparent return to the American System as a blatant bid for western support for his presidential campaign.

Deciding to return to the Senate, in 1845 Calhoun accepted a standing offer by South Carolina senator Daniel Huger to retire in his favor. Once back in the Capitol, Calhoun promptly put his presidential campaign in jeopardy. A dispute between the United States and Great Britain over the northern boundary of the Oregon Territory threatened to start a war. Popular sentiment throughout the United States, spurred on by the slogan "Fifty-four forty or fight!" ran strongly in support of President Polk, who insisted on setting the border at 54 degrees, 40 minutes north latitude, well within modern-day British Columbia.

Calhoun opposed the president on the ground that the United States could not risk a war with Great Britain while tensions were running high in Mexico over the annexation of Texas. Jeopardizing his support both nationwide and in his home state, Calhoun led a successful fight for a compromise that set the U.S.-Canadian border at 49 degrees north latitude, its current location.

Calhoun's success cost him the support of the land-hungry West. His fears of a war with Mexico, however, were borne out. In May 1846, a dispute between the United States and Mexico over the location of the southern boundary of Texas ignited when the Mexican Army attacked an American cavalry unit inside the disputed territory. Calhoun placed himself once more in the opposition. He feared that any conquest of new territory from Mexico would reopen the bitter sectional debate over slavery. Because many of the vast southwestern territories that the United States stood to gain from the war were unsuited to slavery, Calhoun foresaw their becoming new free states, which would destroy the precarious balance of power between the free and slave states in the Senate.

Calhoun continued to oppose the war even after a string of American victories raised patriotism across the nation to a fever pitch. His fear that the war would revive the issue of slavery in the territories was confirmed when, a few months after the war began, David Wilmot, a Democratic congressman from Pennsylvania, introduced a resolution to ban slavery from all Mexican conquests. Calhoun wrote his daughter Anna Maria that he hoped the South would rally together to defeat the so-called Wilmot Proviso. His letter poignantly revealed his divided loyalties: "If [the southern states] regard their safety they must defeat [the Wilmot Proviso] even if the union should be rent asunder. I desire above all things to save the whole; but if that cannot be, to save the portion where providence has cast my lot, at all events."

On Friday, February 19, 1847, Calhoun rose in the Senate to offer a series of resolutions opposing the Wilmot Proviso. He openly declared his loyalty to the South: "There is my family and my connections. There I drew my first breath; there are all my hopes. I am a planter—a cotton planter. I am a Southern man and a slaveholder—a kind and merciful one, I trust—and none the worse for being a slaveholder. I say, for one, I would rather meet any extremity upon earth than give up one inch of our equality—one inch of what belongs to us as members of this great republic!" The resolutions repeated Calhoun's now-familiar arguments that southern security depended on a balance of free and slave states in the federal government, a balance that would be destroyed if the Wilmot Proviso passed.

Calhoun successfully blocked the passage of the proviso in the Senate. His struggle against the war, however, cost him the presidency. He had placed himself in opposition both to most of his own party and to public opinion throughout the South and Northwest. Senator Dixon H. Lewis of Alabama wrote sadly that if Calhoun had not opposed the war, "all the politicians in the country could not have kept him from being President." After finally running out of patience with Calhoun's constant opposition, President Polk dealt him a final blow by reading him out of the Democratic party.

Calhoun made a last desperate bid to achieve his dream in the spring of 1847. At a huge rally in Charleston he called for the South to unite, regardless of party, around a southern candidate who would protect their interests. His plea fell on deaf ears. By the end of the year, Calhoun had resigned himself to defeat. He wrote to a supporter, "All that remains for me is to finish my course with consistency and propriety."

In February 1848, the Treaty of Guadelupe Hidalgo ended the Mexican War. The United States gained California and all the territory between it and Texas. The inevitable battle over slavery in the new territories began, however, not with the Mexican conquests but with Oregon. No one on either side of the issue expected slavery to take root in the far Northwest, but when a bill for organizing a territorial government in Oregon came before Congress in the summer of 1848, both sides saw it as a chance to set a vital precedent for the Mexican territories.

Calhoun argued that Congress, as the representative of the sovereign states, held the territories in trust for them and should therefore guarantee the property rights of their citizens. In addition, he insisted that the northern states should silence their abolitionists. He was infuriated when a new senator, Stephen A. Douglas of Illinois, responded with some truth that what gave the abolitionists their strength was "the speeches of Southern men, representing Slave States, going to an extreme, breathing a fanaticism as wild" as any antislavery leader.

When Congress voted to organize a territorial government for Oregon with a constitution prohibiting slavery, Calhoun considered calling a convention of the southern states to plan a response. He chose to wait, however, for the outcome of the presidential race of 1848. He had decided that, for the nation's next president, he preferred "any respectable southern planter whatever to any man of northern birth and residence."

The Democratic candidate, Lewis Cass of Michigan, was a northerner. The Whig candidate, however, was General Zachary Taylor of Louisiana, a hero of the Mexican War and

Calhoun's daughter Anna Maria Calhoun Clemson sits for a portrait with John Calhoun Clemson and Floride Elizabeth Clemson, two of her four children, about 1848. Even after she married and left home in 1838, Anna stayed in constant touch with her adored father, exchanging a steady stream of letters crammed with gossip, politics, advice, philosophy, and family jokes.

a slaveholding planter. Calhoun briefly considered campaigning for Taylor, but decided that to rejoin the Whigs would be politically unwise. As it turned out, the Democratic party split over the slavery issue. A splinter group of free-soil Democrats, led by Van Buren, took enough votes away from Cass to give Taylor the victory.

The strain of successive battles in the Senate had made Calhoun's precarious health take a turn for the worse. In the spring of 1849, shortly after Taylor's inauguration, he returned to Fort Hill. In April, with the help of his son John, he began a "water cure," which involved lying still for an hour and a half every day wrapped in a damp sheet and buried under heavy woolen blankets, a process he described as "soothing and pleasant."

Calhoun saw himself as the only person who could save the South from destruction by northern interests. He hoped that by producing a reasoned defense of his views he could persuade enough northerners to join the southern cause, thereby saving the Union from disruption. He therefore devoted his remaining energy to completing two books he had begun writing in 1843. Calhoun completed the first, *Disquisition on Government*, before he returned to Washington in December 1849. He never quite finished the second, *Discourse on the Constitution of the United States*.

Published in 1851, the two works are regarded today as the best defense ever written of states' rights and of a strict interpretation of the Constitution. In the *Disquisition*, Calhoun proposed protecting the rights of minority groups within a democracy by establishing government on the basis of a "concurrent," rather than an absolute, majority. Each major interest group in a country must have veto power over the actions of the central government. "By giving to each interest, or portion, the power of self-protection," he wrote, "all strife and struggle between them for ascendancy is prevented."

In *The Discourse on the Constitution*, Calhoun argued that the Constitution as framed by the Founding Fathers contained the concurrent principle. Only in the House of Representatives, with its membership based on population, did the absolute majority rule; minority groups found protection in the Senate, the White House, the Supreme Court, and the process of amending the Constitution.

However, Calhoun continued in the *Discourse*, the intent of the Founding Fathers had been perverted to allow rule by the absolute majority. The imminent destruction of the balance of power between the northern and southern states and the creation of a northern sectional party threatened to impose the rule of the absolute majority on all branches of the federal government. Unless this trend was reversed, monarchy or disunion would be the result.

As he feverishly worked to complete his books, Calhoun found his nightmare of northern domination coming closer to reality. To the stunned chagrin of many slaveholders, President Taylor leaned for support on Senator William H. Seward, the leader of the antislavery faction of the Whig party in New York. Calhoun appealed for a convention of the southern states. In October, 1849, Mississippi called for its sister states to meet in convention in Nashville, Tennessee, in June 1850.

While these events were unfolding, California began to move ominously onto the center stage. The Gold Rush of 1849 had swelled California's population to the point where the territory's military government was no longer adequate to keep order. California's citizens had drafted a constitution prohibiting slavery, which threatened the balance of power in the Senate that many southerners regarded as their last line of defense. President Taylor proposed bypassing the normal territorial stage of government and bringing California directly into the Union with its own constitution. Outraged, Calhoun and other southerners threatened secession. The stage was set for the sectional crisis of 1849–1850, the most serious in the young nation's history.

"Sun of Intellectual light & liberty,
stand ye still, in Masterly inactivity,
that the Nation of Carolina may continue
to hold Negroes & plant Cotton till the
day of Judgment!"

*Calhoun commands progress (pictured as a printing press) to stand
still so "the nation of Carolina may continue to hold Negroes &
plant cotton till the day of Judgment." Published in New York after
Calhoun's 1850 Senate speech—his last—the caricature both mocks
the South Carolinian and suggests the awesome power he wielded
over the South.*

9

"The Poor South!"

IN NOVEMBER 1849, Calhoun returned to Washington for the opening of Congress. He was still frail from his bout with pneumonia—even the short trip between his boardinghouse and the Capitol exhausted him—but he had no intention of missing the Senate's California debate. More days than otherwise, he struggled up Capitol Hill and took his seat in the chamber.

Two weeks into the session, Calhoun suffered a relapse. He recovered slowly, remaining largely confined to his rooms until February 18. During his absence, the Senate began to move slowly toward compromise. On January 29, 73-year-old Henry Clay, who had returned to the Senate after an absence of seven years, submitted a series of resolutions admitting California to the Union as a free state as part of a general settlement of all grievances between the North and the South.

Clay's compromise offered the North more than Calhoun was prepared to give. The South Carolinian felt that he had to convince the northern states that a united South would secede from the Union if its rights were not respected. Accordingly, he began dictating a speech, aimed both at persuading the uncommitted southern states to join his movement for southern unity and at convincing the North that the Union was in mortal danger.

On March 2, Daniel Webster paid a call on Calhoun in his sickroom. Despite decades of battles, the two men maintained a high degree of mutual respect. According to biographer Coit, Calhoun felt Webster to be one of the few men in the Senate who understood him intellectually. Webster for his part later told his friend and biographer, Peter Harvey, that he considered Calhoun to have been "much the ablest man in the Senate, in fact, the greatest man that he had known through his entire public life." After reading a preview of Calhoun's speech, Webster concluded sadly that the desperately ill South Carolinian would indeed reject Clay's compromise and that he spoke for a South about to secede from the Union.

When Calhoun appeared in the Senate on March 4 and sat silently wrapped in his cloak as Senator Mason read his speech, his colleagues saw that he was nearing his end. The next day, when he returned to the Senate and faced harsh criticism by Senator Henry Foote of Mississippi, a moderate southerner in favor of the compromise, feelings of sympathy for Calhoun ran high. Even one of his bitterest enemies, Senator Thomas H. Benton of Missouri, called Foote a "coward."

On March 7, Calhoun was once again in his seat, this time to hear Webster endorse Clay's resolutions and appeal for toleration from both the North and the South. He argued that the geography and climate of the territories conquered from Mexico made them unsuitable for slavery, that an act of God had prohibited slavery in them and that an act of Congress was therefore unnecessary. He denied again, as he had in his debate with Calhoun over the Force Bill, that the Union could be dissolved. Calhoun interjected, "No, Sir, the Union can be broken." Webster replied that it could only be broken by revolution, not by any constitutional procedure. A few minutes later, the final debate between the two men ended.

Calhoun appeared in the Senate for the last time on March 13. After a brief argument with Foote, two friends helped

This symbolic painting, Union, *celebrates the Compromise of 1850, the preservation of the Union, and the American midcentury's three political giants: Clay (seated, center), Calhoun (standing, center), and Webster (standing, right center).*

him out of the chamber. According to witness Varina Davis, the wife of Senator Jefferson Davis of Mississippi, the Senate rose as a body and stood silently as Calhoun left the chamber.

The South Carolinian returned to his deathbed despairing of any solution that might save the Union. "Nothing short of the terms I propose can settle [the dispute] finally and permanently," he wrote his son-in-law. "Indeed, it is difficult to see how two peoples so different and hostile can exist together in a common Union." In a conversation with Senator Mason, Calhoun predicted the coming Civil War with remarkable accuracy:

> The Union is doomed to dissolution and there is no mistaking the signs. . . . I fix its probable occurrence within twelve years or three Presidential terms. You and others of your age, will probably live to see it; I shall not. The mode by which it will be is not so clear; it may be brought about in a manner that none now foresee. But the probability is it will explode in a presidential election.

To Robert B. Rhett, a former Congressman and Calhoun campaign operative, Calhoun burst out despairingly, "The South! The poor South!" Early on the morning of March 31, 1850, he refused all medicine and gave final instructions for the disposition of his papers and personal effects. His son John, one of the attending physicians, heard him say, "I am now perfectly comfortable." A short time later, at 7:15 A.M., Calhoun died.

A battle quickly erupted between the members of Calhoun's family and his admirers in South Carolina over whether the great statesman's body should be buried at Fort Hill or in Charleston. Charleston won, and after resting three weeks in the Congressional Cemetery, Calhoun's casket began its journey south. When the funeral procession arrived in Charleston on April 25, a military guard escorted it through Citadel Square to City Hall, accompanied by the sound of tolling church bells. After lying in state for a day, Calhoun was buried on April 26, in the cemetery of St. Philip's Church.

Calhoun's death was met across the country, even by those who disagreed with him, with a sense of great loss. He had been a national institution for an entire generation of Americans. Southern newspapers gave vent to the widespread fear that without their protector in the Senate the South was doomed. The *Southern Literary Messenger* wrote, "Calhoun has been for a long series of years, the great and almost sole bulwark between the Union and its dissolution. He stood between the living and the dead, and for a time arrested the plague." Many moderate southerners felt, however, that with Calhoun gone, the road lay open for a compromise that would give the Union a new lease on life.

Their predictions were borne out in September, when President Millard Fillmore signed into law the Compromise of 1850, which was based on the Clay resolutions. The compromise bill defused the California crisis. The Nashville Convention, called in response to Calhoun's appeals for southern unity, denounced the compromise and asserted the right of the southern states to secede, but disbanded without taking any serious action.

Calhoun was vindicated, however, in his prediction of civil war. The Kansas-Nebraska Act of 1854 reopened the dispute over slavery in the territories by allowing settlers to decide the issue for themselves. The resulting controversy destroyed the Whig party, led to a vicious civil war between abolitionist and proslavery settlers in Kansas, and gave birth to a new free-soil party, the Republicans.

Three years later, the Supreme Court, in its landmark *Dred Scott v. Sanford* decision, fueled the growing national rift by declaring that slaveholders could not be denied the right to take their property into the territories. When Abraham Lincoln won the presidential election of 1860 at the head of the Republican party, South Carolina was the first southern state to secede from the Union. The jubilant citizens of Charleston celebrated by unfurling a huge banner bearing Calhoun's likeness. After the first shots of the Civil War were fired in Charleston harbor, the Confederate States of America put Calhoun's image on its money.

The defeat and destruction of the Confederacy did not reduce Calhoun's status as a southern folk hero. His body was dug up and hidden to avoid its desecration by Union forces. In 1884, it was removed from its temporary grave and installed in an imposing monument paid for by the state of South Carolina. Northern attitudes towards Calhoun, however, reflected the triumphant nationalism of the victors. The first scholarly biography of Calhoun, Hermann E. von Holst's *John C. Calhoun* (1882), depicted the southern statesman as one of the main forces behind a conspiracy to destroy the Union in order to preserve slavery.

Efforts have been made during the 20th century to rehabilitate Calhoun. William M. Meigs's two-volume *The Life of John C. Calhoun* (1917) emphasized Calhoun's contributions to government and political theory rather than his role as a defender of slavery. The trend continued after World War II, particularly in the works of Charles M. Wiltse and Margaret L. Coit, whose *John C. Calhoun: An American Portrait* (1950) won a Pulitzer Prize.

The Calhoun revival reached its peak during the 1950s and 1960s, when several political theorists and historians presented the South Carolinian as one of the most important contributors to American constitutional theory. These "neo-

Calhounites" saw Calhoun's doctrines of nullification and the concurrent majority as alive and well in the workings of American political parties and in the power exercised over American government by special interest groups.

Ironically, it was a northern politician, Senator John F. Kennedy of Massachusetts, who summed up the views of the neo-Calhounites in 1957 while serving on a committee that named Calhoun one of the five outstanding senators of the past. Kennedy called Calhoun "the most notable political thinker ever to sit in the Senate, whose doctrine of concurrent majority has permanently influenced our political theory and practice."

During the same period, however, Calhoun's theories surfaced in a cause that closely resembled the one in whose defense they were originally developed. Opponents of the integration of blacks and whites in American society used them to justify opposition to the forced desegregation of schools and other public facilities by the federal government.

The debate over the relevance of Calhoun's life and thought for modern times continues. But despite the ongoing controversy, Calhoun's life and career remain an image of tragedy. By choosing to employ his genius in the defense of slavery, Calhoun allied himself with a doomed institution and allowed the presidency to slip from his grasp. His efforts to protect his beloved South made its fate more certain by polarizing the country and by providing a theoretical justification for secession.

In 1865, shortly after the Confederate general Robert E. Lee surrendered his army to the Union general Ulysses S. Grant at Appomattox Courthouse, Virginia, the poet Walt Whitman, while nursing Union wounded in a hospital tent outside Washington, overheard a pair of Union soldiers give Calhoun perhaps his most fitting epitaph. One soldier remarked that he had seen Calhoun's monument in Charleston. The other, a veteran, replied, "That you saw is not the real monument. But I have seen it. It is the desolated, ruined South."

His marble hand resting on the Constitution, his fiery gaze forever fixed on the future, John C. Calhoun seems ready to fight on. With his death, the South lost its most articulate representative and fiercest defender; it also lost part of its own heart. In a sense, Calhoun was the South, and his people knew it. "He fell," said Senator James Mason of Virginia, "a martyr to the great and holy cause to which his life has been devoted—the safety and equality of the Southern States."

Further Reading

Capers, Gerald M. *John C. Calhoun, Opportunist: A Reappraisal.* Gainsville: University of Florida Press, 1968.

Coit, Margaret L. *John C. Calhoun: An American Portrait.* Boston: Houghton Mifflin, 1950.

Current, Richard N. *John C. Calhoun.* New York: Washington Square Press, 1966.

Green, Constance M. *Washington, Village and Capital, 1800–1878.* Princeton: Princeton University Press, 1962.

Meigs, William M. *The Life of John Caldwell Calhoun.* 2 vols. New York: G. E. Stechert, 1917.

Niven, John. *John C. Calhoun and the Price of Union.* Baton Rouge: Louisiana State University Press, 1988.

Peterson, Merrill D. *The Great Triumvirate.* New York: Oxford University Press, 1987.

Von Holst, Hermann E. *John C. Calhoun.* (American Statesmen Series) New York: Chelsea House, 1980.

Wiltse, Charles M. *John C. Calhoun.* 3 vols. New York: Bobbs-Merrill, 1951.

Chronology

1782	Born John Caldwell Calhoun on March 18 near Abbeville, South Carolina
1802	Graduates from Moses Waddel's academy; enters Yale College
1804	Graduates from Yale College; attends Litchfield Law School
1807	Admitted to South Carolina bar; establishes private law practice in Abbeville
1808	Elected to South Carolina state legislature
1810	Elected to U.S. House of Representatives
1811	Marries Floride Bonneau Colhoun; makes his first important speech in Congress, denouncing antiwar speech by Virginia's representative John Randolph
1812	Introduces resolution for war with Great Britain
1817	Appointed secretary of war
1821	Announces his presidential candidacy
1824	Fails in bid for the presidency; elected vice-president under John Quincy Adams
1828	Secretly authors *South Carolina Exposition and Protest*; elected vice-president under Andrew Jackson
1831	Writes Fort Hill Address, stating support for nullification
1832	Resigns as vice-president; elected by South Carolina legislature to U.S. Senate
1843	Resigns from Senate to run for president
1844	Fails in second bid for the presidency; becomes secretary of state
1845	Returns to the Senate
1850	Makes final speech before the Senate
1850	Dies on March 31 in Washington, D.C.

Index

Huger, Daniel, 43, 95

Indians, 19, 21, 22, 48, 52, 53, 60

Jackson, Andrew, 54, 55, 56, 61, 62, 67, 68, 69, 71, 84, as president, 73–82
Jefferson, Thomas, 31, 35, 39, 40, 73

Kansas-Nebraska Act of 1854, 104

Leopard, 42
Lincoln, Abraham, 105
Long Canes, South Carolina, 19–22, 34
Louisiana Purchase, 31

McDuffie, George, 75, 76
Madison, James, 48, 52, 58, 59, 73
Martineau, Harriet, 84
Mason, James, 16, 17, 102, 103
Mexican War, 13, 97
Monroe, James, 59, 60, 62, 65, 71, 75

National Republicans, 73, 76
New England, 29, 31, 41, 52, 71
New Orleans, Battle of, 54, 67, 68

North, the, 14, 15, 17, 71, 72, 88, 101, 102

Pakenham, Sir Edward, 55
Polk, James K., 86, 88, 89, 95, 96
Presbyterianism, 19, 30, 41

Randolph, John ("Mad Jack"), 48, 50, 51, 70
Reeve, Tapping, 35–39
Republican party, 105

Sawney, 26, 91
Senate, U.S., 11, 14, 15, 16, 17, 68, 70, 80, 81, 84, 86, 88, 95, 96, 98, 99, 102
Slavery, 13, 14, 16, 23, 26, 80, 82, 83, 84, 86, 87, 88, 91, 95, 96, 97, 98, 99, 102, 104, 106
Slave trade, 14, 82
South, the, 13, 15, 17, 26, 56, 59, 72, 83, 87, 88, 94, 96, 97, 98, 101, 102, 103, 106
South Carolina, 12, 19, 20, 21, 23, 43, 52, 60, 71, 73, 76, 77, 79, 80, 82, 86, 91, 95, 105
South Carolina Exposition and Protest, 72, 75, 76, 79
South Carolina Piedmont, 20, 23, 26, 42
Spanish Florida, 61, 62
States' rights, 75, 82, 98

Supreme Court, U.S., 99, 105

Tariffs
  1824, 69
  1828, 72, 75
  1832, 76, 79
Taylor, Zachary, 11, 13, 97, 99
Tecumseh, 53
Texas, 15, 86, 87, 88, 95, 97
Tyler, John, 86, 87

Union, the, 11, 13, 14, 16, 17, 31, 73, 75, 86, 87, 98, 99, 101, 102, 103, 104, 105
United States, 13, 15, 32, 42, 51, 52, 53, 56, 61, 62, 70, 80, 86, 88, 95, 97

Van Buren, Martin, 70, 71, 72, 73, 74, 75, 80, 84, 85, 86, 88, 89, 98

Waddel, Moses, 24, 26, 27
War Hawks, 48, 49, 50, 53
War of 1812, 52, 53, 57, 60
Washington, D.C., 11, 13, 14, 45, 47, 50, 53, 54, 56, 59, 61, 62, 71, 74, 75, 77, 82, 83, 98, 101, 106
Webster, Daniel, 12, 54, 75, 76, 80, 85, 102
Whig party, 82, 84, 85, 86, 98, 99, 105
Wilmot Proviso, 96

Yale College, 27–33, 92

PICTURE CREDITS

American Antiquarian Society: p. 64; Bettmann Archive: pp. 36, 49, 52, 57, 63, 94, 100, 107; Collection Mr. Creighton Lee Calhoun, Sr., photo courtesy South Caroliniana Library: p. 18; Clemson University Libraries, Clemson, South Carolina: p. 46; Collection High Museum of Art, Atlanta, purchase with Henry B. Scott Fund: p. 33; Fort Hill, Home of John C. Calhoun, Department of Historic Houses, Clemson University, Clemson, South Carolina: pp. 45, 92, 97; Library of Congress: pp. frontispiece, 10, 12, 15, 16, 20, 22, 28, 48, 55, 68, 71, 73, 74, 77, 81, 82, 85, 87, 90, 103; Courtesy of the Litchfield Historical Society: pp. 38, 40; The New York Public Library, Astor, Lenox, and Tilden Foundations: p. 35; South Caroliniana Library: pp. 25, 78, 93; Virginia State Library: p. 50; Yale University: p. 30; Yale University Art Gallery, Gift of John Hill Morgan: p. 66

Warren Brown, a native of Texas, is currently a graduate student in medieval and American history at the University of Cincinnati. His other titles for Chelsea House include *The Search for the Northwest Passage* in the WORLD EXPLORERS series, *Robert E. Lee* in the WORLD LEADERS—PAST & PRESENT series, and *Colin Powell* in the BLACK AMERICANS OF ACHIEVEMENT series.

Vito Perrone is Director of Teacher Education and Chair of Teaching, Curriculum, and Learning Environments at Harvard University. He has previous experience as a public school teacher, a university professor of history, education, and peace studies (University of North Dakota), and as dean of the New School and the Center for Teaching and Learning (both at the University of North Dakota). Dr. Perrone has written extensively about such issues as educational equity, humanities curriculum, progressive education, and evaluation. His most recent books are: *A Letter to Teachers: Reflections on Schooling and the Art of Teaching*; *Enlarging Student Assessment in Schools*; *Working Papers: Reflections on Teachers, Schools, and Communities*; *Visions of Peace*; and *Johanna Knudsen Miller: A Pioneer Teacher*.